Three things are to be looked to in a building: that it stand on the right spot; that it be securely founded; that it be successfully executed.
— Johann Wolfgang von Goethe

That the Pentagon turned out as well as it did may have been a surprise to its creators. Initially, at least, they did not believe that it was being built at the right place. Generals Eugene Reybold and Brehon B. Somervell and George Bergstrom, the first chief architect of the building, all testified that the designated site was not the right spot; they feared that the structure would not be securely founded because of the hazards of building on the Potomac River flood plain. Nevertheless, the site proved to be on the right spot and close to the seats of government power—the White House and the Capitol. Moreover, the same men who questioned the site and doubted whether the building could be securely founded on it nevertheless saw to the successful execution of the construction. The structure offers visual testimony that it was successfully accommodated to its setting and securely anchored by its strong foundation. And, finally, in more than 50 years of operation it has proved itself a building that indeed has worked well and realized the purpose for which it was intended.

Goethe would have been astonished but pleased.

The Pentagon
The First Fifty Years

Alfred Goldberg

Historical Office
Office of the Secretary of Defense
Washington, D.C.
1992

Library of Congress Cataloging–in–Publication Data

Goldberg, Alfred, 1918–
    The Pentagon: the first fifty years/Alfred Goldberg, p. cm.
    Includes bibliographical references and index.
    1. Pentagon (Va.)–History. 2. United States–Armed Forces–
    Management–History–20th century. I. Title.
    UA26. V8G65   1992
    355.6'0973–dc20   92-20946
                                                                                               CIP

For Sale by the Superintendent of Documents, U.S. Government Printing Office, Washington, D.C. 20402

Foreword

There is a hint of destiny in the coincidence of the end of the Cold War and the fiftieth anniversary of the Pentagon Building. It was in response to the coming of World War II and the enormous military requirements it imposed that, in the 16 months between September 1941 and January 1943, the War Department conceived and constructed the Pentagon as the headquarters building of the U.S. Army. Since the National Security Act of 1947 created a unified military establishment, the Pentagon has served as the Department of Defense command post for all U.S. forces around the world. Throughout those years from 1947 until the present, the Cold War was the major influence on U.S. national security policy and the size, composition, deployment, and operations of the armed forces. Because of the central role of the Department of Defense as a principal guarantor of U.S. national security, the Pentagon has been a symbol of strength and protection to the nation.

A strong U.S. military establishment remains a must, for disorder and instability in the world will not disappear, nor will danger to American security and vital interests. It is essential in the uncertain international environment ahead that the Pentagon be able to fulfill its function of safeguarding the nation no less effectively during the next half century than it has in the past 50 years, and, it is to be hoped, with much less expenditure of the nation's resources.

Dick Cheney

Preface

I first saw the Pentagon in February 1943, less than a month after its completion. As I drove by on the highway I identified it immediately, even though I had never seen a picture of it. It was not until October 1945, on my return from military service in Europe, that I entered the building. I remember being more impressed by the great distances of the interior than by the grand scale of the exterior. Since 1946 I have spent many working years in the building and have witnessed the many changes that have occurred in it. Accordingly, some of the information and many of the comments about the building and its operation derive from my personal observations over a period of almost half a century. My visual examinations of the structure, its functions, and its inhabitants became much more frequent and acute once I undertook research for this book. I looked at the building—inside and outside—with a new eye and a keener awareness. I saw things I had never before seen. Some I shall never see again, for the renovation of the building planned to begin in 1995 will make radical changes, eliminating and altering many familiar features.

The Pentagon has had a busy life during which it matured and changed, probably more than most buildings. Its role as a symbol and as the center of the U.S. military establishment is well known and has been the subject of a prolific literature. This book addresses the building itself—its origins and its construction, and how it has changed during the first half century of its existence. It may also dispel some of the myths and misinformation about the Pentagon that have been common for many years. Finally, it may inspire greater appreciation of the remarkable feat of conception, design, and construction achieved by the planners, architects, engineers, builders, and workmen who created the building.

Many agencies and people helped to make this undertaking possible. L. Walter Freeman, Director for Real Estate and Facilities of OSD's Washington Headquarters Services, suggested the desirability of observing the Pentagon's 50th anniversary by publishing a history of the building. He and his staff, including Jerry R. Shiplett, Elbert R. Humphrey, and David W. Callin, were responsive at all times in providing information and offering comments on drafts of the manuscript. David O. Cooke, Director of Administration and Management, encouraged initiation of the project and supported it wholeheartedly throughout its preparation.

At the Office of History, Headquarters Army Corps of Engineers, at Fort Belvoir, Va., Martin K. Gordon provided access and guidance to the valuable records on the Pentagon in that office's collection. Others who made information available were John Taylor and Edward Reese of the Military Reference Branch at the National Archives, Deborah Weissman of the General Services Administration, Laura Dodt and Hugh Howard of the Pentagon Library, and Daniel Koski-Karell.

Pictures came from many sources—the National Archives, the Library of Congress, the Pictorial Services Office of the Assistant Secretary of Defense for Public Affairs, the OSD Historical Office, U.S. government and other publications, and especially the Witmer Collection, presented to the government by Peter Witmer. Through the good offices of Betty Sprigg of Pictorial Services, Robert Ward and Helene Stikkel photographed many scenes in and around the building at my request. Kathleen Brassell of the OSD Graphics Office developed the concept for the design of the book and oversaw its completion. Kelly Jamison and Kyle McKibbin displayed infinite patience and great skill in executing the design and layout of the book.

Reviewers of the manuscript made many helpful suggestions for corrections and changes that clearly resulted in a more coherent and better organized product. For this improved result I am indebted to Thomas R. Brooke, Alice Cole, Vernon E. Davis, Robert L. Gilliat, Lawrence S. Kaplan, Ronald Landa, Richard Leighton, Maurice Matloff, Stuart Rochester, and Robert J. Watson. Finally, Ruth Sharma, who meticulously transcribed and helped edit and critique numerous drafts, is deserving of special thanks for her gracious forbearance during what must have seemed to be an interminable process.

ALFRED GOLDBERG

Contents

Introduction 1

I. Conception and Construction 3

II. Pentagon Profiles 93

    Architecture 97

    Cost 111

    Possible Alternative Uses 115

    Ownership and Operation 117

    Structural Changes 119

    Dedicated Corridors 125

    Amenities 131

    Inside Vehicles 137

    Transportation 139

    The National Military Command System 143

    Security 149

    Demonstrations 153

    Inhabitants 157

    Pentagon Lore 175

    Environmental Impact 177

Conclusion 181

Appendixes 182

Note on Sources and Bibliography 193

Charts

1. Organization of the War Department—June 1941 6
2. The Army on the Eve of Pearl Harbor 42
3. Organization of the Army (The Marshall Reorganization) 9 March 1942 63
4. Office of the Secretary of Defense—15 September 1948 118
5. Department of Defense—June 1991 161
6. Office of the Secretary of Defense—August 1991 166

Illustrations

War Department building in Philadelphia 4
War Department building in Washington 4
State, War, and Navy Building 5
Munitions Building 8
New War Department Building 8
Under Secretary of War Patterson and General Somervell 11
Secretary of War Stimson and General Marshall 13
Early sketch of pentagonal design 15
Flooding on Hoover Airport site 17
Original sketch of Pentagon Building 18
General Somervell 21
President Franklin D. Roosevelt 23
Senator Alva Adams 25
Pentagon and environs 26
John McShain, Clarence Renshaw, and Henry Thompson 29
Pentagon planning principals 30-31
Home of the architects 32-33
J. Paul Hauck 35
David Witmer 37
Engineer Office staff, Pentagon 38-39
Architects and draftsmen 41
Model of the building 45
Harold L. Ickes 46
Building location plan, 1942 47
Preparing the site 48-49
Early site preparation 48-49
Washington orientation of the Pentagon 50-51
A long haul 52-53
Building site, 15 September 1941 55
Construction progress on Section A, November 1941 57

Floor plan guide	59
Schematic drawing, 1942	61
Leslie R. Groves	62
Plan of road system	64-65
New road and overpasses	67
Interior of heating and cooling plant	68
Exterior of heating and cooling plant	69
Shift change, 1941	71
Construction progress, December 1941	72
Architects and draftsmen in hangar	73
Front of Section A, December 1941	74
Design staff members	74
Early 1942 view	75
Section A, January 1942	76
Section B, February 1942	77
View from Navy Annex, March 1942	78-79
Telephone switchboard	80
Center Court construction, May 1942	81
Four Sections, June 1942	82-83
Section A, November 1942	84-85
Clarence Renshaw	86
Preparing the tunnels, November 1942	87
River Entrance view, November 1942	88
High aerial view	90
Mall Entrance and Center Court	91
River Entrance, spring 1990	94-95
Mall Entrance, 1990	96
River Entrance and Lagoon	97
River Entrance Ceremony	101
Center Court, c. 1950	102
Program in Center Court, 1946	103
Original Cafeteria, 1942	104-105
Cafeteria, 1991	106
Center Court, 1992	107
Five Capitol Buildings	109
River Entrance, 1990	110
John McShain	113
File room	114
James Forrestal	116
David O. Cooke	117
Open bay "Busy Bees"	119
Pentagon helicopter pad	120
View of Concourse	121
Bus tunnel	123

POW/MIA Corridor	124
Eisenhower Corridor	125
Hall of Heroes	126
NATO Corridor	127
MacArthur Corridor	128
World War II Paintings Corridor	129
Pentagon Library	130
Concourse, c. 1960	131
Library scene	132
Crystal City backdrop	133
Child Development Center	135
Concourse construction, 1942	136-137
North Parking	140-141
National Military Command Center	142
Robert S. McNamara	143
Current Action Center	145
Emergency Conference Room	146-147
Joint Staff entrance	148
Entrance from Metro underground	151
Anti-Vietnam War demonstration, 1967	152
1967 demonstration	155
General George Marshall	156
Fire drill, River Entrance	159
Directors of Women's Services	162
Unification cartoon	163
Secretary of Defense office	164
Frank Knox	165
Richard B. Cheney	167
General Colin L. Powell	167
Ceremony for King Saud	168
President-elect Eisenhower at Pentagon	169
Robert A. Lovett and Winston Churchill	170
George Marshall and Anna Rosenberg	171
President Truman with Louis A. Johnson and General Omar Bradley	172
James Forrestal and military department secretaries	173
River Entrance	174
South Entrance, 1990	176
Rosslyn skyline	178
Crystal City skyline	178-179
Pentagon City	179

The Pentagon
The First Fifty Years

WAR · DEPARTMENT

FRANKLIN · D · ROOSEVELT
PRESIDENT · OF · THE · UNITED · STATES · OF · AMERICA

HENRY · L · STIMSON
SECRETARY · OF · WAR

ROBERT · P · PATTERSON
UNDER · SECRETARY · OF · WAR

GENERAL · GEORGE · C · MARSHALL
CHIEF · OF · STAFF

LT · GEN · BREHON · SOMERVELL
COMMANDING · SERVICES · OF · SUPPLY

MAJ · GEN · EUGENE · REYBOLD
CHIEF · OF · ENGINEERS

MAJ · GEN · THOMAS · M · ROBINS
CHIEF · OF · CONSTRUCTION

BRIG · GEN · LESLIE · R · GROVES
DEPUTY · CHIEF · OF · CONSTRUCTION

LT · COL · CLARENCE · RENSHAW
DISTRICT · ENGINEER

G · EDWIN · BERGSTROM
DAVID · J · WITMER
CHIEF · ARCHITECTS

JOHN · McSHAIN INC
DOYLE & RUSSELL
WISE · CONTRACTING · CO INC
BUILDERS

J · PAUL · HAUCK
BUILDERS · MANAGER

Introduction

Three buildings housing great institutions of the U.S. government have come to be regarded as national monuments and have become part of national and international history: the White House, the Capitol, and the Pentagon. Like the Vatican, the Kremlin, and the Houses of Parliament in London, they have acquired a distinct public character as symbols of government, and their names evoke worldwide recognition.

If there were seven wonders of the modern world comparable to the seven wonders of the ancient world, the Pentagon would surely be among them. Of the seven ancient wonders only one survives: the Pyramids of Gizeh, which took scores of years to build and are now more than four thousand years old. The modern wonder—the Pentagon—was built in 16 months, and after 5 decades of existence must undergo a complete renovation of its interior.

The Pentagon is three in one: It is a building, an institution, and a symbol. It is an engineering marvel—a product of its times and civilization. Born of necessity, built in great haste, and occupied section by section, it turned out to be a much better building than anyone expected or had a right to expect. In appearance and soundness of structure it exceeded expectations. It is doubtful that any building of comparable size and utility has been constructed before or since or so expeditiously.

The institutional status of the Pentagon derives from its role as nerve center of the country's armed forces—the largest of U.S. government institutions. From 1942 to 1947 it housed the War Department and since then the major elements of the Department of Defense (except for the Marine Corps): the Office of the Secretary of Defense, the Joint Chiefs of Staff, and the highest echelons of the headquarters staffs of the Army, Navy, and Air Force. From the Pentagon the president and the secretary of defense have exercised worldwide command and control of the country's armed forces.

A symbol to the nation and the world since its beginning, the Pentagon above all is a metaphor of American power and influence with all the good and bad images such a symbol suggests. For most Americans, it is the embodiment of U.S. strength and authority, the nerve center of the military establishment, a rock of security. To others it is a symbol of militarism and violence, a "temple of death." Over the years the traditional antimilitary instinct of the country has given way to acceptance of the Pentagon as a necessary bulwark in a violent and unstable world.

The Pentagon has also symbolized the enormous growth and influence of the military establishment in a country with an enduring antimilitary tradition. At the time of its construction in 1941-43, President Franklin D. Roosevelt and most of the government and the public believed that the building was a response to temporary circumstances and that it would not be required for the military after the war, when conditions would return to normalcy. But the post-World War II world did not return to what Americans regarded as normalcy. Much of it remained in flux, frequent, convulsive changes occurred, and the country encountered persistent and powerful threats to the security of the United States and its friends. Hence, the compulsion to maintain large military forces that averaged almost 2.5 million between 1945 and 1990, nearly 8 times as much as before 1940.

This required a much larger military structure in Washington, of which the Pentagon became the flagship with the creation in 1947 of the National Military Establishment, retitled Department of Defense in 1949. Strong consensus on the necessity to provide for security against threats was always tempered by the hope that the need for such large military forces would be short-lived.

Even before it was completed the Pentagon entered history. From the time it became public knowledge that it was to be built, it excited attention and comment, initially only in Washington but eventually throughout the land. During its construction there evolved a miscellany of fact, fiction, myth, whimsy, illusion, and fantasy from which came a folklore of humor, black humor, and hostility that still endures after half a century. Indeed, the lore grew by accretion over the years. After 50 years it is time to set the record straight.

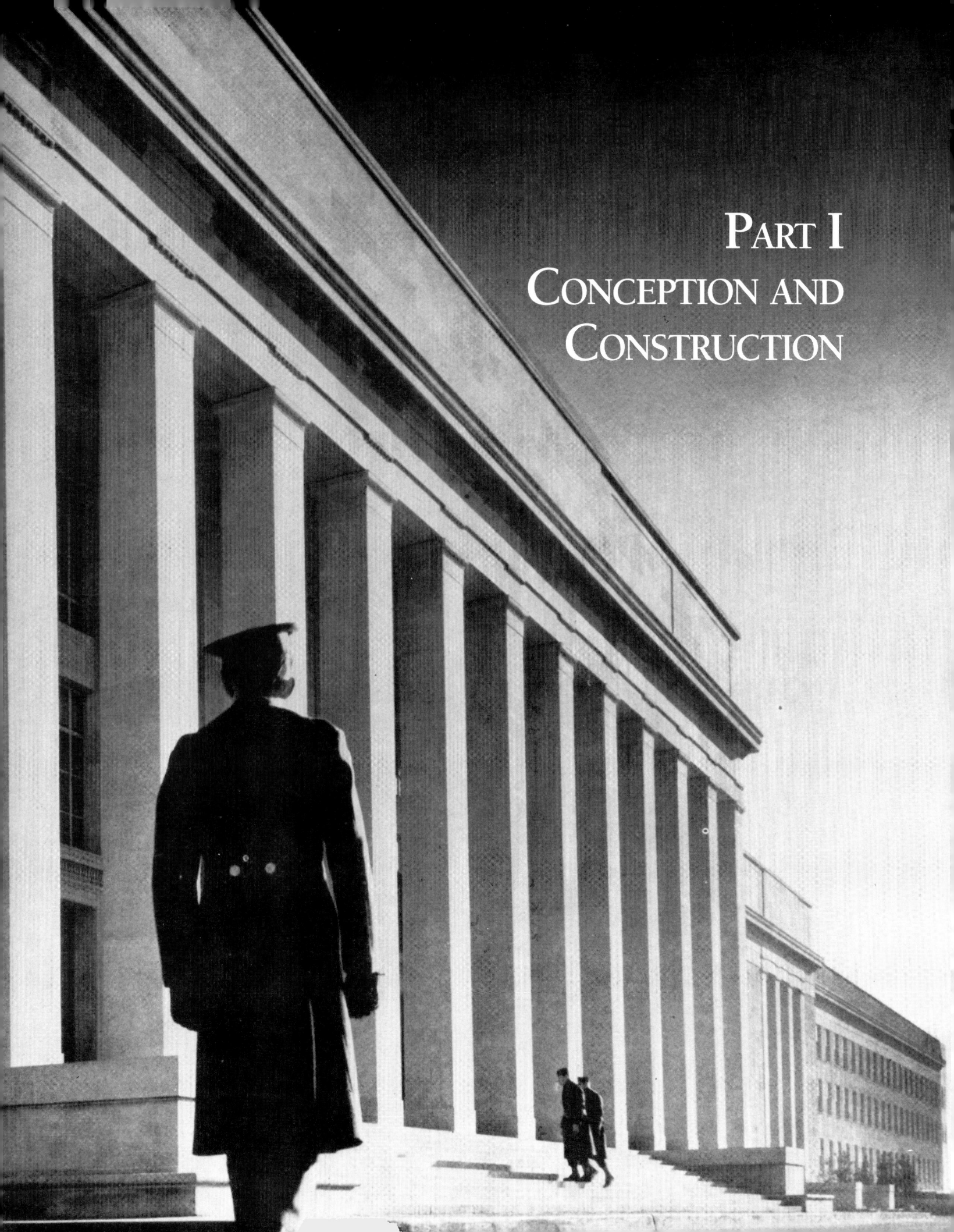

Part I
Conception and Construction

The War Department occupied this modest house at 5th & Chestnut Streets, Philadelphia, then the nation's capital, from 1797 to 1800

From 1820 to 1879, this War Department building stood at 17th St. & Pennsylvania Ave., N.W., Washington, D.C.

Toward the end of August 1939, only days before the German invasion of Poland on 1 September detonated World War II, Secretary of War Harry H. Woodring and the Acting Chief of Staff of the Army, General George C. Marshall, moved their offices into the austere Munitions Building on Constitution Avenue, already inhabited by much of the Army staff. The departure of these last two War Department offices from the ornate French neoclassical-style State, War, and Navy Building, immediately to the west of the White House on Pennsylvania Avenue, marked the end of 60 years of occupancy there by War Department offices. The stay of the department's top leadership in the Munitions Building would be much briefer.

The home they had left, the State, War, and Navy Building, now known as the Old Executive Office Building, cost more than $10 million and was reputed at the time of its completion in 1888 to be the finest and largest office building in the world, "covering, together with lawns and terraces, more than five acres of ground space." Erected on a site occupied by buildings that had housed the War and Navy departments since 1820, it was almost 17 years in the making. As the first wings of the new structure were completed the War Department moved out of the old Northwest Executive Building which was then razed to make room for additional wings. Curiously, the number five had a special significance for the State, War, and Navy Building as it did much later for the Pentagon—it had five wings and five stories, and it stood on five acres of ground.

The State, War, and Navy Building, completed in 1888

By contrast, the Munitions Building was a "tempo," a temporary building constructed during World War I and completely without ornamentation, inside or outside. Here the top officials of the War Department remained for more than three years, during which they labored intensely to prepare the United States to wage the war that seemed likely to engulf it and that came, indeed, on 7 December 1941.

After the lightning German conquest of Poland in September 1939, there followed more than seven months of so-called "Phony War" or "Sitzkrieg" during which British and French armies confronted German armies across their respective fortifications—the Maginot Line and the Westwall. The German invasion and occupation of Norway and Denmark in April 1940 set off alarm bells in Washington, but it was the smashing German blitzkrieg victories over the French and British in May and June and the fall of France that shocked the U.S. government into taking immediate action to rearm the nation against potential and increasingly potent enemies.

A partial mobilization of U.S. manpower and industrial resources began in the summer of 1940. For the Army this meant a planned tenfold increase in its strength and the provision of camps, airfields, and munitions on a huge scale. Call-up of National Guard and reserve units and individuals and the Selective Service System provided the manpower. In Washington the War Department headquarters staff proliferated feverishly to cope with its vastly expanded responsibilities. As a consequence, efforts by the National Capital Parks and Planning Commission to rid the scenic Mall of World War I temporary buildings came to a complete halt by autumn when the War Department was demanding more buildings, not fewer. By the summer of 1941 the Army had grown from a force of about 270,000 only a year before to more than 1.4 million men, including 630,000 draftees and more than a quarter million National Guardsmen, and was adding more daily.

In the Washington area, the War Department had 24,000 military and civilian employees in 17 buildings, most of them in the District of Columbia. The Munitions Building, with 779,000 sq. ft. of space, was the largest.

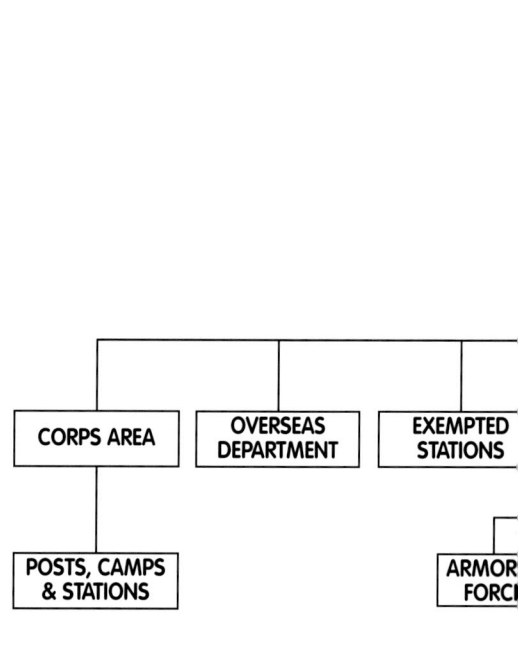

In Virginia, the department occupied some facilities at Fort Myer in Arlington and in Alexandria. Department buildings in Washington included apartment houses, garages, warehouses, and residences, most of them occupied beyond normal capacity. The Office of the Inspector General was in an apartment house; the Adjutant General's Office had only 45 sq. ft. (5' x 9') per person. Cramped conditions and wide dispersion did not make for efficiency.

In all, the department occupied 2.8 million sq. ft. of space, of which 350,000 sq. ft. went for records. The shortage of office space alone was estimated at 734,000 sq. ft., and a still greater shortage could be counted on because of an anticipated 25 percent increase in personnel by 1 January 1942. An additional 300,000 sq. ft. was also needed for record storage.

Chart 1

ORGANIZATION OF THE WAR DEPARTMENT
JUNE 1941

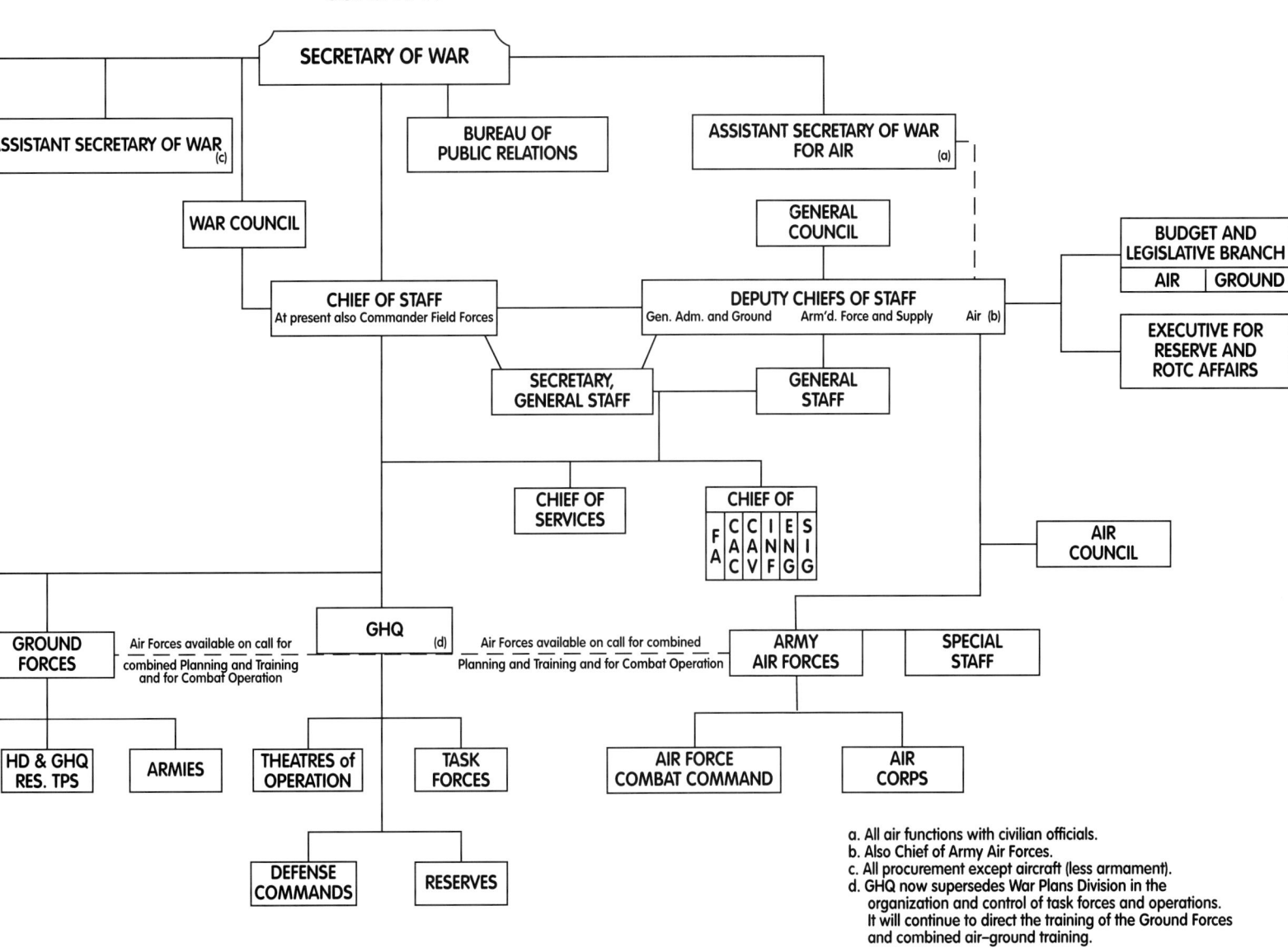

a. All air functions with civilian officials.
b. Also Chief of Army Air Forces.
c. All procurement except aircraft (less armament).
d. GHQ now supersedes War Plans Division in the organization and control of task forces and operations. It will continue to direct the training of the Ground Forces and combined air-ground training.

Munitions Building, Constitution Ave. & 20th St., N.W., built shortly after start of World War I

New War Department Building, 21st & C Sts., N.W., planned in 1938 as War Department headquarters

Completion in June 1941 of the New War Department Building* at 21st and C Sts., N.W., in the Foggy Bottom area, intended as a replacement for the Munitions Building, permitted increased flexibility in the allocation of space for a short time. When Secretary of War Henry L. Stimson inspected the new $18 million building in April he was impressed by its "500,000 square feet and 260,000 square feet of office," but so swiftly did the mobilization progress that within a month Stimson told the president that still more space would be needed for the department. Opened in June 1941, the building could house only the Office of the Under Secretary of War and the Office of the Chief of Engineers.

The continued breakneck expansion of the Army to meet ever higher goals meant that the Washington headquarters would also continue to grow until it would greatly exceed the capacity of the buildings occupied by or available to the War Department. And given the possibility that the United States might find itself at war at almost any time, the pressure for additional space would remain critical, indeed overwhelming. In and around Washington, there was little or no office space to be found.

The unceasing demands for space, far exceeding the desperate efforts to meet them, required a bold solution. A bold man and a bold idea provided the solution—a single building that would house the whole War Department staff and its appendages in the Washington area.

The man behind the Pentagon Building was Brig. Gen. Brehon B. Somervell, a dynamic, ruthless, impatient, and above all decisive Corps of Engineers officer who served as chief of construction for the War Department. Somervell, a 1914 West Point graduate, had a meteoric rise to high rank and important position during World War II. As Chief of the Construction Division of the Office of the Quartermaster General beginning in December 1940, Somervell's responsibility for building cantonments for the rapidly expanding Army extended to the construction of buildings in Washington. Promoted to brigadier general in January 1941, he became assistant chief of staff G-4 of the War Department General Staff in charge of Army logistics in November and advanced to major general in January 1942. On 9 March 1942 he was appointed commanding general of the Services of Supply** with the rank of lieutenant general. It was an impressive rise from colonel to lieutenant general in 15 months. In 1940 Somervell had asked General Marshall for a field command; instead, he received "the biggest headache in the War Department"—the Construction Division. It proved to be an unusually rewarding headache.

Like some other Engineer officers engaged in civil works, Somervell had acquired political acumen and excellent political connections, above all with Harry L. Hopkins, a particularly powerful and influential figure in the Franklin D. Roosevelt White House. Hopkins held a series of major government appointments over a period of a decade, including administrator of the Works Progress Administration (WPA), secretary of commerce, and administrator of Lend-Lease. He had the confidence and ear of the president, and for two and a half years during the war he lived in the White House in a small suite near the Oval Office, a rare and unusual arrangement.

* The Department of State took over the building in 1947 and added an extension in 1956-61 that was four times as large as the original section.
** Redesignated Army Services Forces in 1943.

On occasion Hopkins represented the president abroad in direct talks and negotiations with such world leaders as Winston Churchill and Joseph Stalin. Churchill, who esteemed him highly for his critical judgment, referred to him as "Lord Root of the Matter." Hopkins had interested himself in defense matters over the years and strongly supported the rearmament programs that began in 1938.

As WPA administrator in New York (the largest WPA unit in the country) between 1936 and 1940, Somervell had worked for Hopkins and earned his respect and friendship. The Hopkins connection gave Somervell access to the White House and the president, and he was not averse to taking advantage of it. Moreover, Somervell was perceived in Washington as an officer clearly on the rise, and this lent added weight to his advice and decisions. An astute and knowledgeable observer of the Washington scene, Rexford G. Tugwell, spoke of Somervell as "one of the most remarkable of all of the figures of World War II . . . . For cutting red tape and getting things done there had never been anyone like him."

Under Secretary of War Robert P. Patterson and General Brehon B. Somervell, 1945

The summer of 1941 was one of great anxiety and apprehension in Washington. Fears for the survival of Great Britain, which had stood alone against Germany for a year after the collapse of France, diminished after the German invasion of the Soviet Union on 22 June, but the possibility, many thought probability, that the Soviets would fall created new fears. With the whole European continent under Adolf Hitler's domination, would it be possible for Britain to stand alone against him? Through the Lend-Lease Act of March 1941 the United States sought to strengthen British defenses, and it subsequently extended this munitions assistance to the Soviet Union.

It seemed to the American military that Hitler, once master of Europe, would move into Africa from where he could pose a direct threat to Latin America, and in turn menace the United States. The American defense perimeter then would have to include the whole Western Hemisphere, a daunting prospect. In some South American countries, German agents were already engaged in political and economic activities that appeared to be aimed against U.S. interests. To help secure the North Atlantic lifeline to Great Britain and to guard against any German attempt to seize Iceland, U.S. troops started to move into the island on 7 July. In September, the United States undertook to protect all shipments from American ports to Great Britain as far as Iceland.

Events in the Far East further contributed to the tension and foreboding in Washington. As the Japanese drive for control of China and Southeast Asia continued unabated, the threat to U.S. interests in the Pacific area could not be ignored. And as relations between the two nations grew steadily worse, the United States caused further strain by initiating economic sanctions. It was against this backdrop of violent, earthshaking events, and in an atmosphere of pervasive uncertainty and feverish preparation for the worst eventuality, that Somervell advanced his bold concept of a single building that would serve as the nerve center of a huge Army (and Army Air Forces) that might have to fight on most of the continents of the world.

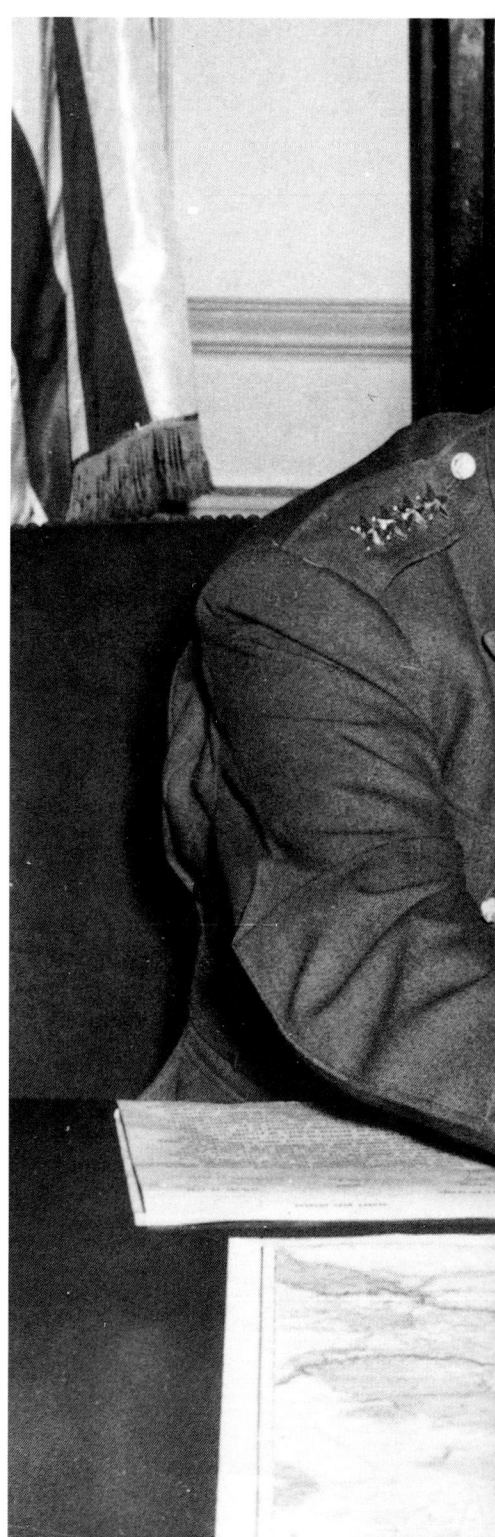

*Secretary of War Henry L. Stimson
and General George C. Marshall, 1942*

Somervell's decision to push for a single monumental building accorded with previous intimations of interest in that direction from both the War Department and Congress. Two years earlier, in his report to the secretary of war for fiscal year 1939, the then Chief of Staff, General Malin C. Craig, had broached the possibility. He pointed out that the department's activities were housed in 20 widely dispersed buildings and that this made for delays that "are embarrassing in peacetime and may be inadvisable in the event of even a relatively minor emergency." Accordingly, the "need for the erection of a main building unit which will permit the grouping of all agencies in a central location continues to be a primary consideration. The successful conduct of war is predicated upon prompt decision and coordinated execution. A major war would demand the immediate regrouping of the primary activities of the War Department in a single building." By July 1941 a major emergency had come and a major war was on the horizon.

Earlier, in May, the Public Buildings Administration had proposed construction of temporary buildings for the War Department and other agencies in suburban areas of the city. The War Department had been considering a number of sites, including two in the District—one near Walter Reed Hospital in northwest Washington and one in the area of the Army War College (later Fort Lesley J. McNair). Chief of Staff General Marshall rejected the latter site because it was in an already overcrowded area in southeast Washington. Sites in Maryland, regarded as too remote from the seats of power in Washington, received little consideration. A close-in Virginia site in Arlington had many advantages: the government already owned much land there and could acquire more at reasonable prices, transportation would be easier outside of Washington, and ample parking could be provided.

For some months, then, in the spring of 1941 Marshall had been looking for a site where the department could erect a complex of large temporary buildings to house the proliferating staff. An Arlington site appealed to him. Congress had authorized funds for the construction of temporary buildings, but it had specified that they should be built in Washington. On 11 June in testimony before the House Appropriations Committee Marshall asked that limitations on construction outside of the city be removed so that the former Arlington Farms experimental agricultural site in Arlington could be used for construction of temporary office buildings. Marshall considered the site exceptionally convenient, "about 4 minutes from the War Department" just across the Memorial Bridge and readily accessible to downtown Washington and other government buildings. "To be able to build our temporary office buildings on the Arlington farms site means everything to us; we can do business if our buildings are placed there."

The site that appealed to Marshall had been acquired by the U.S. government as part of a much larger tract from the heirs of Robert E. Lee in 1883 for $150,000.* Arlington Experimental Farms, between Arlington National Cemetery and the Potomac River, had been established on about 400 acres of this land, transferred from the War Department by act of Congress in 1900. In November 1940 Congress had shifted jurisdiction over a large tract of Arlington Farms from the Department of Agriculture back to the War Department and authorized the latter to acquire additional land needed for military purposes.

---

* This land had been acquired in 1778 by John Parke Custis, a stepson of George Washington. Custis's granddaughter, Martha Ann Randolph Custis, married Robert E. Lee and brought the estate with her into the Lee family.

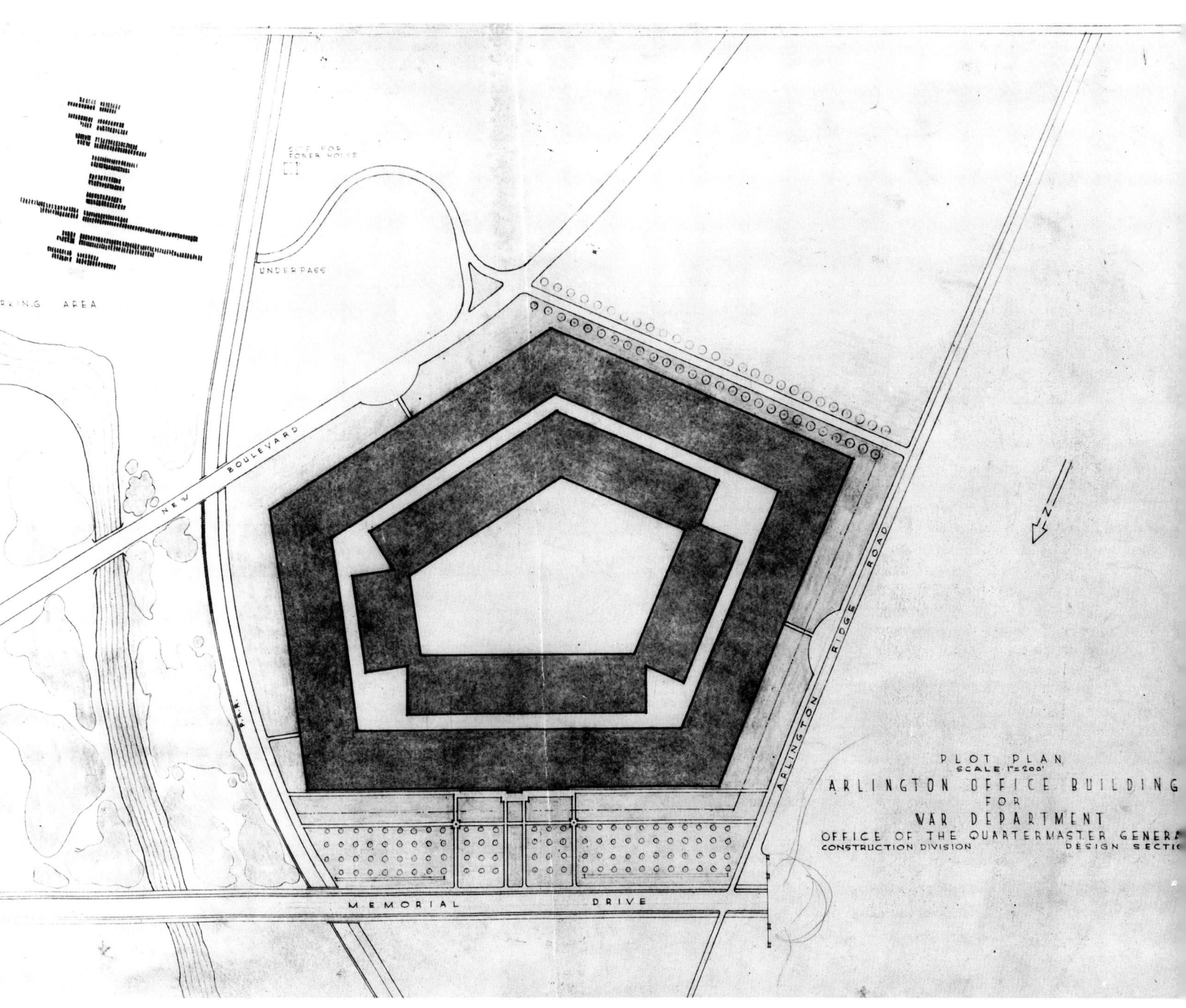

Early sketch of pentagonal design at Arlington Farms site

As chief of the Construction Division, Somervell had been wrestling with the problem of finding sites and constructing buildings for the War Department staff. A site across the Potomac in Virginia seemed preferable to any in the District of Columbia for reasons that seemed eminently cogent to Somervell and other responsible officials in the War Department concerned with the projected new building. Sufficient land for an unobstructed site for a building of the size contemplated did not exist in the preferred federal West Executive area, known also as the Northwest Rectangle and as Foggy Bottom. This tract, on the north side of Constitution Avenue, opposite the Navy and Munitions Buildings and between the new Department of Interior Building at 18th and C Streets and 23rd Street, N.W., had been considered for some time as the prime area for federal construction, and the New War Department Building had been put up there. Traffic in that area was already severely congested, and another large facility would make the situation worse. Nor could adequate parking be provided. Moreover, the provision of services and utilities—heating, air conditioning, water, sewage disposal, gas, electricity, and telephone mains—for such a massive structure would compound existing problems with other buildings in the area. Luther Leisenring, a key member of Somervell's staff, suggested later that the "Pentagon was put in Virginia because if it had been built in Washington it would have come under the Supervising Architect of the Treasury and Somervell would have had little to do with it." Obviously, there were more compelling and pragmatic reasons than this for putting the building in Virginia.

Spurred on by the urgency of the critical space shortage, Somervell put forward the exciting and intriguing notion of housing the entire War Department headquarters under a single roof. In July he presented the idea to the Deputy Chief of Staff, Maj. Gen. Richard C. Moore, himself a Corps of Engineers officer and concerned with Army construction. At Moore's suggestion, Somervell talked with Rep. Clifton S. Woodrum, the Virginia congressman who was chairman of the subcommittee of the House Committee on Appropriations considering construction estimates and likely to be receptive to an Arlington site. Woodrum, who thought well of Somervell, suggested that the War Department adopt a comprehensive plan to solve its space problem. When the Bureau of the Budget request for $6.5 million for temporary buildings in or near the District of Columbia came before the House committee on 17 July, Woodrum suggested that the War Department look toward an overall solution of its space problem.

That same evening, Thursday, 17 July, Somervell set in motion the machinery to carry out the grandiose vision of the largest office building in the world, one that would dwarf even the greatest structures in the capital. He summoned his top engineers and his top architects, principally Lt. Col. Hugh J. Casey, Chief of the Design Section, Col. Leslie R. Groves, Col. Edmund H. Leavey, and George Bergstrom, his chief consulting architect, and gave them oral instructions to provide him by 9:00 a.m. Monday morning, 21 July, basic plans and architectural perspectives for a fireproof, air-conditioned office building to house 40,000 persons. Somervell wanted a building of four stories or less with no elevators; the site would be along the south bank of the Potomac in Arlington, about three-quarters of a mile below the Arlington Farms tract. The land would come from an 80-acre area of the Arlington Cantonment at Fort Myer, intended as the site for a Quartermasters Corps depot, and from the newly acquired 146.5 acres of the old Washington-Hoover Airport.

Casey and Bergstrom proved to be superb choices for the nearly impossible task that Somervell had imposed on them. The former was a brilliant engineer officer with outstanding educational and practical experience. He would have probably played an important part in the design and construction of the new building, but he left Washington for the Philippines in September to become General Douglas A. MacArthur's chief engineer for the Philippine Department. MacArthur asked for Casey personally and although Somervell attempted to persuade him to remain with the Construction Division, he left. He went on to a distinguished career throughout the war as the Chief Engineer Officer for the Southwest Pacific Area. Bergstrom, a notable California architect with outstanding credentials and president of the American Institute of Architects from 1939 to 1941, had become a consultant to Somervell earlier in 1941 and took on the demanding job of chief architect of the Pentagon at age 65. His previous experience had centered on design of large commercial structures—hotels, office buildings, stores, and banks. Among his better known works were the Hollywood Bowl and the Los Angeles Museum of History, Science, and Art.

Flooding on Hoover Airport site

The Chairman of the District of Columbia Commission on Fine Arts, Gilmore D. Clarke, a prominent engineer and landscape architect, who had had a run-in with Somervell some years before, wrote to the Senate Appropriations Committee protesting the "flagrant disregard" of maintenance of the integrity of the Arlington area as an honored national cemetery site and deplored the "introduction of 35 acres of ugly flat roofs into the very foreground of the most majestic view of the National Capitol." The view was the magnificent vista of Washington along the line formed by the Lee Mansion, Memorial Bridge, and the Lincoln Memorial. Subsequently, Clarke testified against the proposed building at a Senate committee hearing and suggested moving it to the more southerly site.

A powerful protest came also from Frederic A. Delano, Chairman of the National Capital Park and Planning Commission and a cousin of President Roosevelt. In a detailed letter to the Senate Appropriations Committee on 31 July on behalf of the commission, he, too, deplored the "permanent" injury that would be done to the "dignity and character" of the area adjacent to Arlington Cemetery and spoke to the "single question of the practicability of the project as a whole." His objections centered on the difficulties of transportation—only 12 percent of the War Department's employees lived in Virginia. Moreover, he recommended halving the size of the building—from a capacity of 40,000 to 20,000. And "last, but not least," he asked, "is it wise to put the entire general and official staff of the Army in one place where many of them might be subject to being put out of action?"

On the previous day, 30 July, Delano and the Director of the Budget, Harold D. Smith, who opposed the project because of its cost, had gone to the White House to present their objections in person to the president. On 1 August Roosevelt wrote to the Chairman of the Senate Subcommittee on Deficiencies, Alva Adams, that he had "no objection to the Arlington Farm" site but agreed with Delano that the building ought to be half the proposed size, initially limited to 20,000 War Department employees. Looking to the future, he confided that it had been his "thought that after the present emergency the Congress would provide the necessary appropriations to complete the planned development of that section lying between Constitution Avenue, E Street and west of 21st Street [the West Executive Area] wherein it is proposed to locate the permanent homes of the War and Navy Departments."

Resistance to the bill held up its passage for a month. The final hurdle in the Senate subcommittee proved to be the designation of the site. The original site, the depot area three-quarters of a mile southeast of Arlington Farms that General Reybold had considered too low-lying, emerged again as a candidate. Somervell and Bergstrom fought efforts to shift the site down the river, arguing that the change would delay the start by a month, and alterations required by the more difficult site and in the design and the need for numerous access roads would make the building more costly, probably at least $5 million more. Moreover, Somervell did not find it unseemly that Arlington Cemetery should overlook the War Department building.

Chairman of the Senate Subcommittee on Deficiencies, Alva Adams

Somervell enlisted the aid of Under Secretary of War Patterson, who wrote to Senator Adams expressing his concern that the depot site, known as Hell's Bottom because of its unsightly shacks, dumping grounds, warehouses, and railroad yards, was "unworthy of the dignity of the department." Patterson and Somervell prevailed; the subcommittee approved the Arlington Farms site to the north, after inspecting both sites. The Senate passed the bill on 14 August after defeating amendments to place the building in the District of Columbia instead of Virginia and to reduce its size by half. The appropriation bill passed by Congress did not prescribe the size or design of the building.

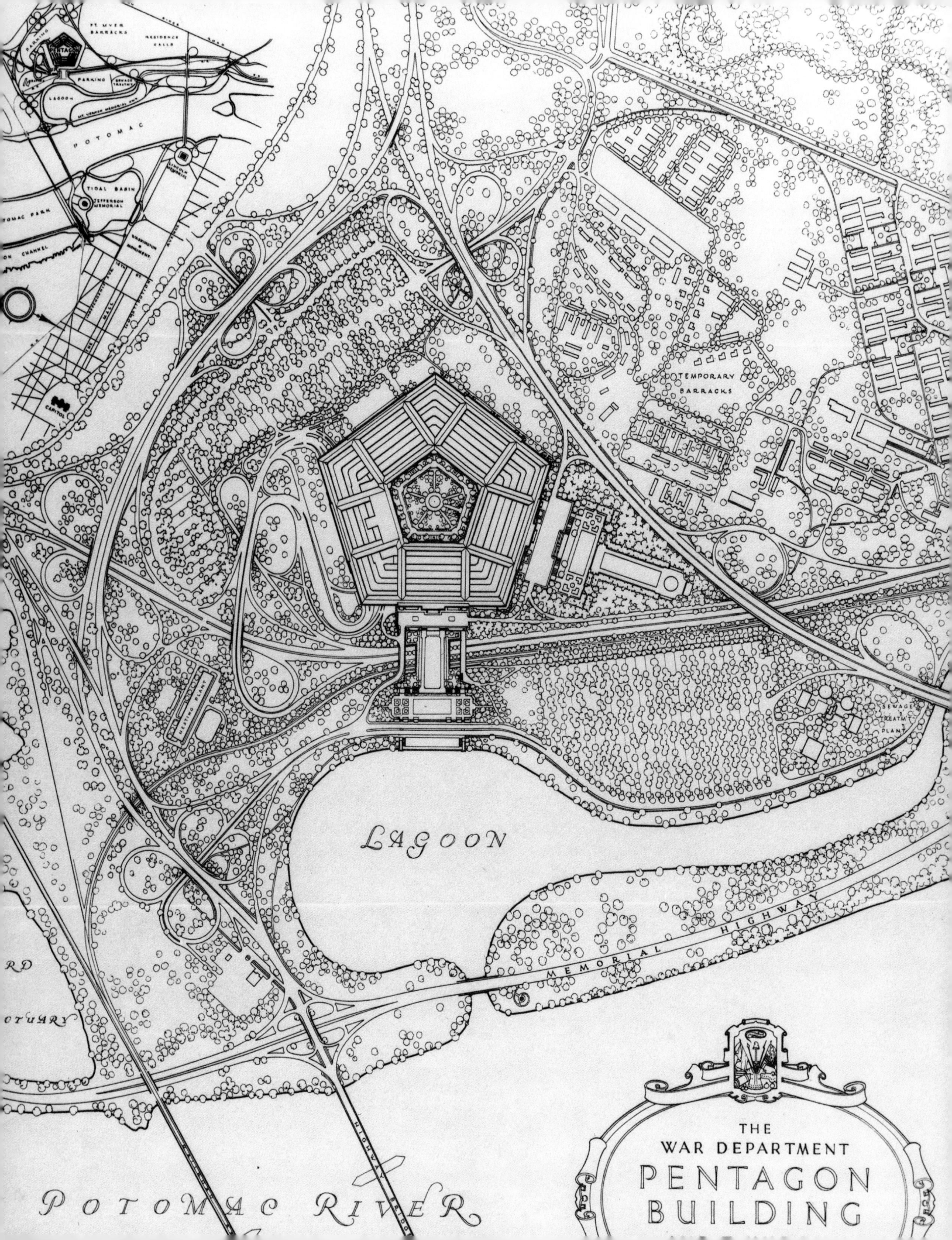

Although the Senate approved the choice, the struggle was not yet over. Planning the building engaged and held the attention of the president himself. Franklin D. Roosevelt had long had a strong interest in and appreciation of architecture and had participated to some degree or other in making decisions about the design and construction of public buildings in Washington. A structure of the scale and purpose of the proposed War Department building could not fail to command his personal involvement from the beginning. During most of August President Roosevelt had had other things than the building project on his mind. He had left Washington for some days to meet with the Prime Minister of embattled Great Britain, Winston Churchill, in what became known as the Atlantic Conference, at Argentia, off the coast of Newfoundland.

Shortly after Roosevelt's return to Washington, Gilmore Clarke succeeded in gaining an appointment with him. Clarke expressed how "bitterly" the National Capital Park and Planning Commission opposed the site and how strongly his own Fine Arts Commission was opposed. According to Clarke, the president replied: "I read your testimony before the Congressional Committee, and I agree with you . . . . I haven't time this morning to go into this, but if you would come down here in about a week we'll go over on the Virginia side and look around and pick a new site for the building."

At a press conference on 19 August Roosevelt proclaimed his disapproval of the Arlington Farms site and spoke feelingly of his part in placing temporary buildings—the Navy and Munitions Buildings—on the Mall during World War I. "It was a crime . . . for which I should be kept out of Heaven, for having desecrated the loveliest city in the world—the Capital of the United States." He mentioned Arlington Cemetery and the view of the city from there and of the proposal "to put up a permanent building, which will deliberately and definitely, for one hundred years to come, spoil the plan of the National Capital . . . . I have had a part in spoiling the national parks and the beautiful waterfront of the District once, and I don't want to do it again." The president spoke of other alternative sites and concluded with the remark that "this building that is proposed on the other side of the river is much larger actually than we need in Washington. Besides which, it spoils the planning of 150 years."

On 20 August Roosevelt, apparently reinforced in his opposition by Clarke's and Delano's objections to the northern site opposite Memorial Bridge, called Somervell and Assistant Secretary of War John J. McCloy to the White House and vetoed the Arlington Farms site. He ignored Somervell's objections that the move would increase the cost of the building. In signing the appropriation bill on 25 August, the president announced he reserved the right to pick the location. The same day he informed a press conference that a building half the size planned would be constructed at the depot site. The president hoped the building could be used after the war to store records, and that the War Department would then be housed in Washington.

The next day, 26 August, the president summoned Smith, Clarke, Somervell, and Bergstrom to his office and made clear his preference for the southerly site and for a building smaller than Somervell had proposed. He asked those present to prepare an agreement in accord with his directions.

Thus, at the president's behest, Stimson, Smith, and Delano* signed a joint memorandum on 28 August which Somervell sent to the president two days later. They agreed on a building to house 20,000 people at 125 sq. ft. per person to be erected in the area of the depot site. In view of the fact that the War Department might be returned to the District of Columbia after the war, they indicated that "the proposed building should be constructed with sufficient strength for future use to store archives." The president approved the memorandum. On 29 August Roosevelt took Somervell, Clarke, and Smith on a tour of the proposed site. According to Clarke's recollection, Somervell expressed his preference for the Arlington Farms site in such strong terms that the president cut him off with the reminder, "My dear General, I'm still Commander-in-Chief of the Army!" At the depot site Roosevelt pointed to it and said "Gilmore, we're going to put the building over there, aren't we?" To drive the point home to Somervell he said, "Did you hear that, General? We're going to locate the War Department building over there." Somervell could not but agree.

On the way back to the White House Roosevelt asked if Somervell would show the plan for the building to the Commission of Fine Arts. Somervell replied that he did not intend to do so since the building would be in Virginia and therefore outside the sphere of the commission. Provoked by Somervell's stubbornness, Roosevelt commanded him: "Well, General, you show the plans to the Commission of Fine Arts and, when they've approved of them, show them to me." Once more, Somervell had little choice but to obey. It was characteristic of his impatient, hard-driving style that he would resent and resist opposition even from his superiors, including the president, and that he would seek ways of circumventing them in order to have his way. Still, in spite of his strongheaded behavior and his capacity for irritating his superiors, Somervell continued to command the respect and support of Stimson, Marshall, Hopkins, Patterson, and McCloy.

His interest in the building aroused, Roosevelt offered specific suggestions. At the end of a Cabinet meeting the same day as his visit to the site, the president advanced the notion that the building should have no windows, relying on artificial light and ventilation. Of this proposal, Stimson wrote in his diary: "It struck me as so fantastic that I did not express myself to him, but I told Somervell afterwards. . . I should absolutely refuse to live in a building of this type." Stimson was spared making an issue of this because the president agreed to windows when "munitions experts convinced him that a bombing that would demolish solid masonry walls would merely blow the glass out of windows."

* After Delano's subsequent personal appeals to the president failed to stop the project or alter it sufficiently to satisfy him, Delano resigned as Chairman of the National Capital Park and Planning Commission. His letter of resignation conveyed his feeling of frustration: The commission "no longer performed any planning functions; the government agencies to which it had to turn over the land purchased for them usually failed to put it to suitable use." It seemed clear that aesthetic considerations in planning for the nation's capital would have to yield to the pragmatic demands of mobilization for war.

The president's thunderbolts would have devastated a lesser man than Somervell. He had already plunged ahead with his plans for the building, anticipating passage of the appropriation bill. As early as 24-25 July Somervell had selected the contractors—John McShain, Inc., of Philadelphia, and two Virginia companies, Wise Contracting Company, Inc., and Doyle and Russell, both of Richmond. Somervell substituted the two Virginia firms for two New York City companies recommended by the Construction Advisory Committee, perhaps as a gesture to Representative Woodrum for his support of the project. McShain had built the newly opened (16 June) National Airport, the Jefferson Memorial, and part of the New War Department Building in Washington, and was finishing up the Naval Medical Center in Bethesda, Maryland.

Left to right—McShain, Renshaw, Henry S. Thompson, Special Consultant to Office of Chief of Engineers, July 1942

On 19 August Somervell convened the team he had selected to run the project. In addition to Casey and Bergstrom, he brought in Col. Leslie R. Groves, Capt. Clarence Renshaw, John McShain, and others. Groves, who later headed the Manhattan District that developed the atom bomb, exercised oversight of the project until its completion, although he had less time to devote to it after September 1942, when he undertook his atomic duties. A man of great energy, force, and self-confidence, he much resembled Somervell. Renshaw, an experienced and well-trained construction engineer who knew the territory, directed the work of the contractors. He had been in charge of recent construction at the adjacent Arlington Cemetery, including the utility center, approaches to the Tomb of the Unknown Soldier, and restoration of the Lee-Custis Mansion. The new project dwarfed anything he had worked on before.

Somervell told the group that he wanted 500,000 sq. ft. of floor space ready by 1 March 1942 and the entire building finished by 1 September. Bergstrom, as architect-engineer, and Renshaw, as construction chief, reporting directly to Groves, would have charge of the project.

The area selected for the building site—the eastern end of Arlington County, along the south bank of the Potomac River—had a rich historical background. Indians inhabited the region for millennia, beginning about 10,000 B.C., before the first European colonists appeared in the seventeenth century. The earliest published reference to the area is in Captain John Smith's account of his exploration in 1608 of the Chesapeake Bay and its tributary rivers, including the Potomac—*Map of Virginia with a Description of the Country*, published in London in 1612. Smith ascended the Potomac up to the end of tidewater—the present Chain Bridge at the northern end of Arlington County. He received friendly treatment from the natives and took note of an Indian village named Namoraughquend near the present site of the Pentagon. The name is believed to mean "place where fish are caught." It is likely that there were other Indian villages in the vicinity also.

General Somervell and Pentagon planning principals - 1942. Left to right–David Witmer, George E. Bergstrom, Somervell, Col. Leslie R. Groves, Maj. Clarence Renshaw, J. Paul Hauck

European settlers came into the area after 1650, and plantations were established later in the century. The original District of Columbia, which came into existence in 1801, was a square 10 miles by 10 miles and included the Northern Virginia area of Alexandria County (now Arlington County). Thus the Pentagon site was part of the District of Columbia until the federal government ceded the area of approximately 33 square miles back to the State of Virginia in 1846.

By 1860 the area had begun to lend itself to a number of industrial and recreational uses. During the Civil War, this region just across the Potomac River from Washington was heavily fortified by as many as 10,000 Union troops. Forts, camps, and entrenchments covered the landscape down to Alexandria, and the area remained under a military governor until 1870 when it was returned to Virginia.

In the years between the Civil War and World War II the area underwent commercial, industrial, and recreational development, particularly in the form of brickyards and a race track. In 1926 Washington's first municipal airport—a commercial venture named

Home of the architects, June 1942

Hoover Airport—was built in the area of the future Pentagon site. A second airfield—Washington Airport—opened immediately adjacent to it in 1927. In 1930 the two airports were combined and served the city until the opening of Washington National Airport in June 1941. The old airport's demise helped clear the way for the federal government to acquire for $1 million on 10 July part of the land on which to build the Pentagon. The airport made a further contribution to its successor in the form of a surviving Eastern Airlines hangar that was used to accommodate the hundreds of members of the planning and design staff during the construction of the Pentagon.

At a press conference on 2 September Roosevelt announced his approval of the site and the basic scheme for the building: It would be pentagonal, with some 15 wings, and it would accommodate 20,000, not 40,000, employees. Somervell's only public reaction to the president's remarks was to announce that construction would begin within two weeks. But in-house he had to take account of the changes in design and contract that would have to be made because of the president's dictates. Somervell met with his engineers and contractors, including Groves, Renshaw, Bergstrom, and McShain, on 4 September to discuss the problems. Contracts would be negotiated and new estimates prepared. Among the physical changes, floor loads would be 150 pounds per sq. ft. (very high) in the event that the building actually became a record storage facility in the future. There could be no doubt that this would be a permanent building—not a temporary wartime structure. Moreover, Somervell would see to it that the building would not be halved in size as many supposed because of the president's announcements.

John McShain acted as Contractors' Representative by written agreement among the three contractors. This was appropriate since McShain carried by far the greater part of the workload. The arrangement created an embarrassing situation later, in the summer of 1942, when plans were being made to place, at the Mall Entrance, an official marker bearing the names of those responsible for the creation of the building. As originally proposed, the plaque carried McShain's name as Contractor and the other two companies—Doyle and Russell and Wise Contracting Company—as Associated Contractors. The latter two protested vigorously and asserted their legal rights as full partners in the enterprise. They insisted that the names be listed as they were in the contract or that they be omitted entirely. Groves believed that the two Virginia companies had played a minor role in the construction work, but Somervell, more politically sensitive, ruled that the three contractors should be listed equally on the rectangular limestone plaque.

The elements of a design staff for the project had begun to emerge the weekend of 18-20 July when Somervell had first demanded plans and an architectural perspective for the building. At Somervell's direction Bergstrom, as chief architect, assembled during August a separate drafting force to plan the project, working in the basement of a Fort Myer warehouse. As his chief assistant, and later, successor, Bergstrom chose David J. Witmer, a prominent and highly experienced architect from Los Angeles, who directed the detailed design. Witmer had been the chief architectural supervisor for the Federal Housing Administration in Southern California from 1934 to 1938. He came on board on 8 August and succeeded Bergstrom as chief architect on 11 April 1942 after the latter's resignation.* Thereafter, Witmer had complete charge of design and made the important decisions required by the numerous problems that arose during the greater part of the construction period.

* Bergstrom's departure followed by two weeks the termination of his corporate membership in the American Institute of Architects for improper and unprofessional conduct as president of the Institute.

Right, Chief Architect David J. Witmer, October 1942

In addition to this design force, there was established a field force for supervision and inspection that also came initially under the chief architect. Bergstrom explained that the "superintendence and inspection cost is higher [than for other projects] because all sections of the project are very large and will be constructed simultaneously." The supervisory force of six architects from private practice worked under a chief coordinator. Each one served as the supervisory field architect for a particular part of the project—building or grounds— and oversaw the workmanship and the timing of the work. The inspection force under these field architects, organized by trade, had inspectors for excavation, piling, masonry, plumbing, electricity, plastering, heating, air conditioning, roofing, hardware, millwork, etc. This field force added 117 people to the office of the chief architect, making a grand total of 444. Later, the field force came under the supervision of the district engineer, Colonel Renshaw.

The number of major architectural drawings eventually totaled 3,100 and averaged 34" x 60" in size. Since construction went on simultaneously with design and because builders needed information immediately, for periods of time it was necessary to issue drawings every night. Machines for reproducing prints ran 24 hours per day and used an average of 15,000 yards of print paper per week. Weekly output of prints ranged from 12,000 to more than 30,000, and outside blueprinters had to be used at times to meet particularly heavy demands. Even this prodigious output could not always keep up with the demands of the builders; McShain complained about failure of drawings and specifications to meet construction needs. Differences between architects and contractors involved other matters also, including use of other than specified materials.

That design and specification proved to be the principal bottleneck should have occasioned no surprise. Ordinarily, architects on large buildings have many months' start on the contractor. For the Pentagon, an enormously outsized building, Bergstrom, Witmer, and their staff had virtually no lead time. Construction began only weeks after Somervell asked for plans. Pressure on the architects became intense. Sometimes construction actually got ahead of plans and often, by the time specifications for materials appeared, a different material had already been used in the building. The architect in charge of specifications, Luther Leisenring, a long-time Construction Division civilian employee and supervising architect of the division from 1930 to 1941, when Somervell replaced him with Bergstrom, referred to his specifications group as the "historical records" section because it was so often behind actual construction.

Architects and draftsmen at work

The urgent thrust after Pearl Harbor to speed up construction and occupation of the building added greatly to the burden of the harried architectural staff. Renshaw reported to Somervell that the contractors were agreeable to a proposal to make a million square feet of space available for occupancy by 1 April 1942 but that the "chief architect is unwilling to commit himself to such a schedule." He informed Somervell that "it will be necessary for me to take more active control of the architect's activities but I can and will do so."

Chart 2

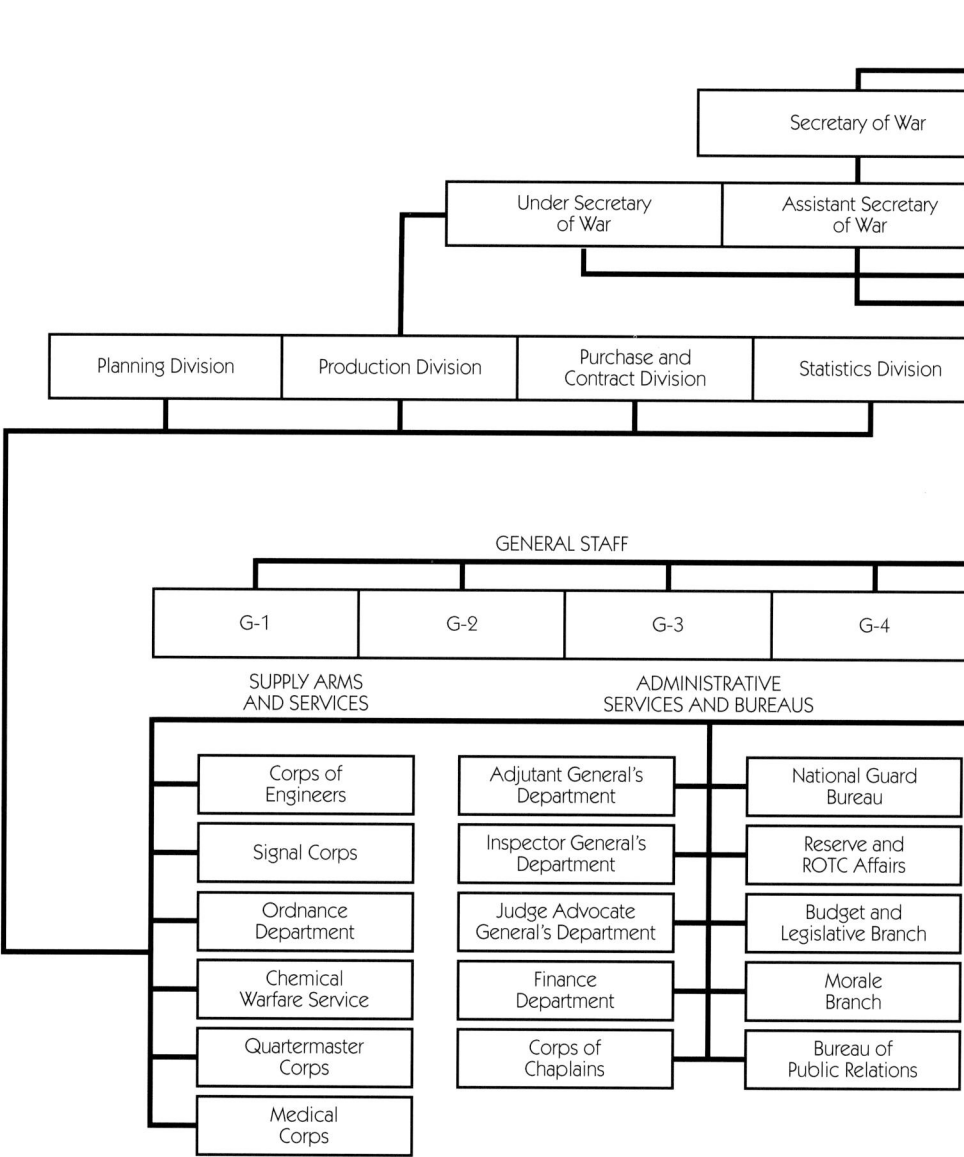

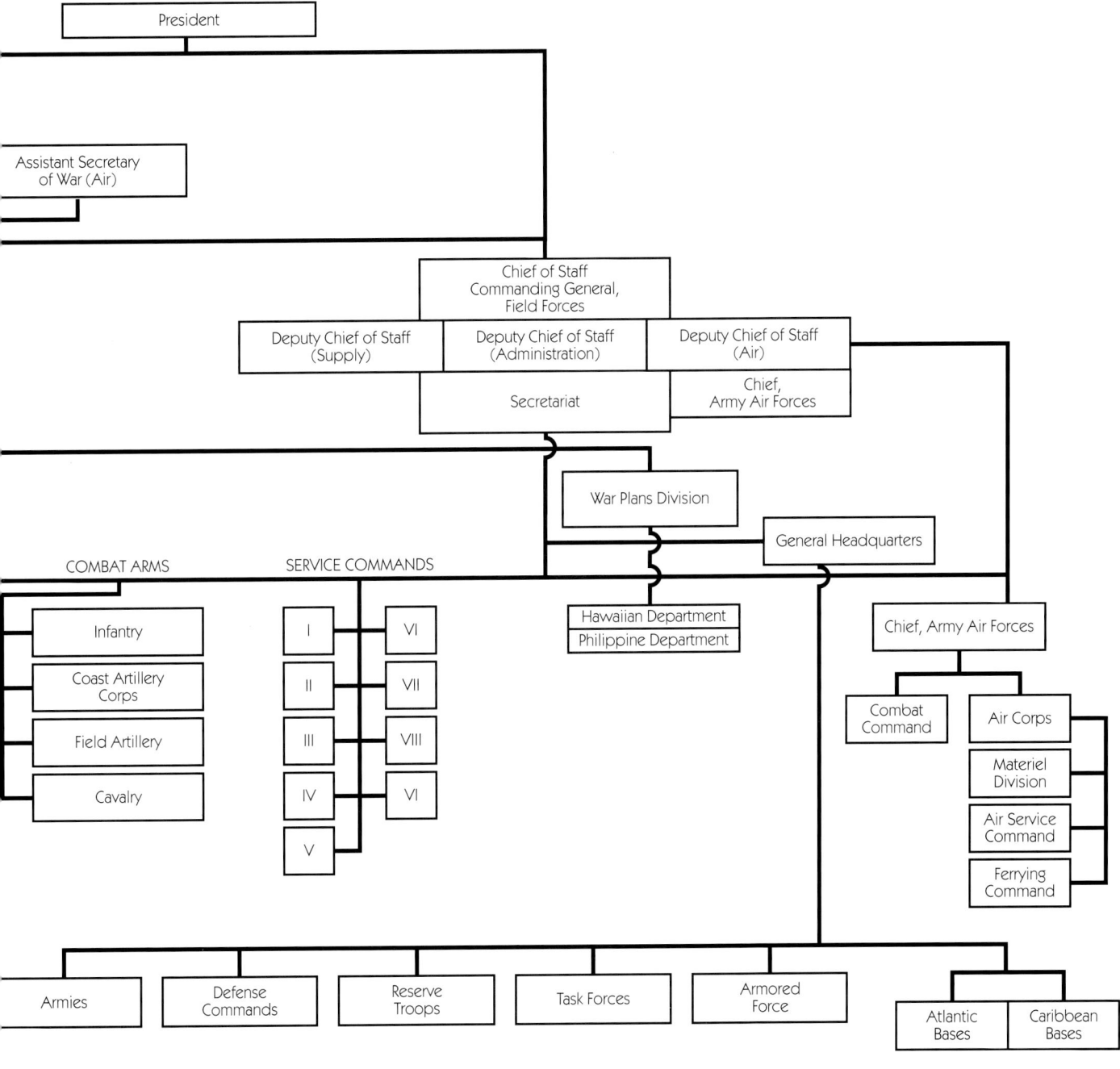

On the Eve of Pearl Harbor

Conception and Construction

Clashes also occurred directly between the builders and the architects. McShain's constant pressure on architects for designs created friction from almost the beginning of construction. The contractor also criticized some of the designers' construction methods and materials specifications. McShain's suggestions about design did not sit well with Bergstrom. At Renshaw's request, Somervell ruled that the contractor was to build the structure in accordance with the architect's design, and Renshaw should see to it that it was so done. The contractor might suggest changes in design or materials that he thought would speed the work and decrease cost. Somervell reserved to himself final decision.

Full-scale work on design of the building had begun on 8 August; 34 days later, by 11 September, groundbreaking day, hundreds of draftsmen and engineers had made 2,500 drawings. On 11 September Bergstrom presented Somervell with two designs of a regular pentagon: one with wings perpendicular to inner and outer perimeters; the other with concentric perimeter rings connected by cross wings. Somervell chose the latter design, which provided quicker movement within the building. Despite the shift in site that occurred, the pentagonal shape was retained. The Fine Arts Commission tentatively approved the plan. Work on designs and blueprints went ahead at a faster clip, and the initial basic drawings were completed by early October.

The original determination in July to shape the building as a pentagon and give it a horizontal rather than a vertical projection remained firm throughout the design process. Thus the decision to limit the height of the building, initially to three or four floors and finally to five as pressure to accommodate more people became stronger. The optimum structure for a building of such giant dimensions, housing so huge a work force, would be one that provided the shortest horizontal travel distances for pedestrians within the building. Since any shape approaching a circle provides the greatest area with the shortest walking distance within (the center of a circle is the nearest point to any spot on the circumference), the ideal structure would be a series of concentric rings intersected by radial corridors tying the rings together. The plan of concentric rings—five rather than two as originally announced (eventually labeled A to E from the innermost ring out)—with light courts between rings, offered daylight for most offices and combined flexibility with concentration of offices and facilities.

In fact, although the president had called for a building to house only 20,000 instead of 40,000, the revised plans provided for a building about four-fifths the size of the original planned for the Arlington Farms site. The complex was to have about 4 million sq. ft. of space, 320 acres of landscaped paths with plazas and terraces, large parking lots, an intricate system of roads, and bus lanes under the building.

Secure in the knowledge that the project was well-launched, Somervell authorized the first public release of information about the new building on 7 October. The release emphasized that the "size, design and location of the building have received the personal attention of the President and the plans as announced reflect the instructions issued to Brigadier General Brehon B. Somervell, Chief of Construction." The building would have three stories and a basement (this counted as four stories since the so-called basement was above ground level), would have the shape of a pentagon, and would have two concentric rings erected around a five-acre landscaped inner court.

Somervell asked to see the president to make a progress report. He went to the White House on 10 October and presented the president with what amounted to a fait accompli. Construction had been going forward for a month, the work force numbered a thousand men, and hundreds of huge concrete piles had been driven into the soil. Somervell predicted a cost of about $33 million and completion of the building in 14 months. Despite his previous reservations, Roosevelt voiced no objections to the proposed size. He imposed one condition—there should be no marble in the building. Somervell suggested a limestone facing to which Roosevelt did not object. Roosevelt continued to take a personal interest in the project throughout the construction period and paid occasional visits to the site.

Model of the building

That a building to house 20,000 people, as directed by the president, should be four-fifths the size of a building intended for 40,000 people provoked some comment. To speculations and allegations that Somervell, determined to have his giant building, had doubled the office space requirement per occupant, thereby justifying the revised plans, the general replied "utterly ridiculous." Self-assured as always, especially having just come from his 10 October conference with the president, he added, "Do you think any Government official in his right mind would fail to conform to the President's orders?" It is not difficult to believe that Somervell could find a way around the president's orders.

At this point another opponent attacked the War Department's construction program, and particularly the Pentagon project. Harold L. Ickes, the caustic, blunt-spoken secretary of the interior, in a vintage Ickes speech to the National Capital Park and Planning Commission on 18 October, more than a month after construction on the Pentagon had begun, charged that the War Department's lack of continuing planning was responsible for "tearing into shreds the carefully worked out plans for the Nation's Capital." He cited as "the outstanding example . . . the sudden construction of another New War Department building in Virginia with its upsetting influences involving shifting populations, traffic congestions, and a general disturbance of the whole city pattern." The president ignored the Ickes blast.

Secretary of the Interior Harold L. Ickes

46   Conception and Construction

The chosen site presented serious difficulties because it was on two levels instead of one. This required major alterations in construction plans. On the west side of the building, the ground was 40 ft. above sea level; on the east side nearer the river, only 10 ft. above sea level. To avoid overflow from the river, the lower level had to be filled to raise it to 18 ft. Along the line where the 40-ft. and 18-ft. levels met, a strong retaining wall had to be built. Since a 22-ft. high retaining wall seemed to be costly and perhaps risky, it was decided to divide the lower area into two levels, a mezzanine and a basement. This required retaining walls at two levels but was regarded as preferable to the single large wall. The basement of the original plan became the first floor of the upper level; these changes resulted in a five-story building for the two outer rings but only four stories for the three interior rings, with a basement and mezzanine under about one-third of it, on the River and Mall sides. The enclosed floor space, originally about 4 million sq. ft., increased ultimately to more than 6 million sq. ft.

Building location plan, 1942

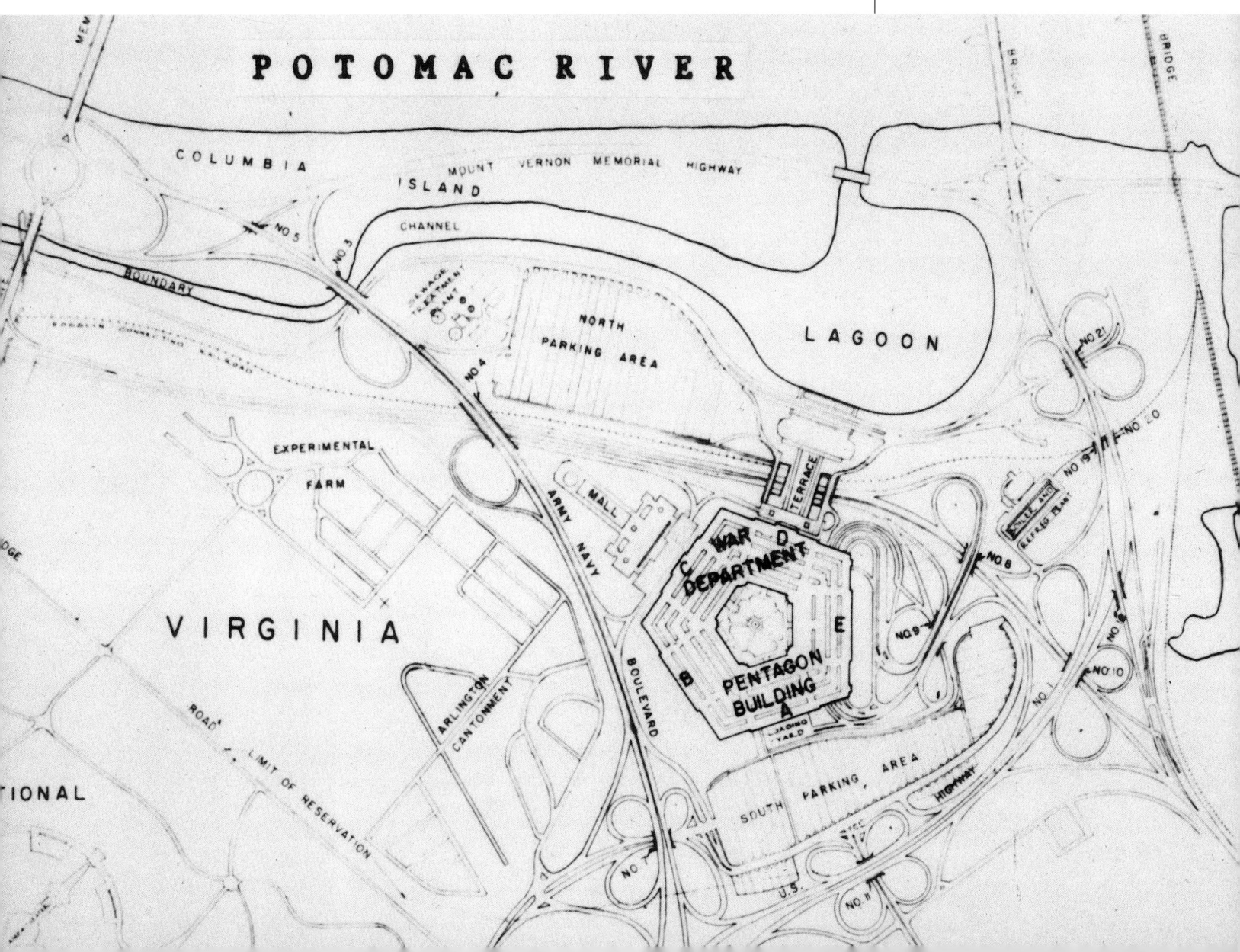

Preparing the site, Arlington Cemetery in background

Early site preparation, Navy Annex in background

Conception and Construction 49

A Corps of Engineers history described some of the materials problems that Somervell and his team had to contend with.

> *Interest in the choice of materials ran high, as competing industries and rival states vied with one another for a share in the prestigious project. Typical of the many letters received by Renshaw was one from a Georgia Congressman, complaining that specifications for granite steps at the entrance limited the choice to North Carolina, Rhode Island, and Maine. Also typical was the CQM's [Chief Quartermaster General] reply: Although Georgia granite would not harmonize with the color of the facade, it might find a place elsewhere in the structure. By far the largest uproar was over the building's 9,000 windows. When invitations went out late in October for alternate bids on steel and wood sash, manufacturers of wood sash promptly cried 'foul,' claiming that the specifications gave steel an edge. A flood of letters and telegrams inundated the War Department. Somervell and McShain wished to ignore the clamor but OPM [Office of Production Management] would not agree; and by 10 November new invitations were in the mail. At an opening on the 18th, steel won out. Although the question was settled, protests continued for weeks.*

The battle over window sash was no small matter, for there were more than 7,700 windows of varying sizes in the building. Most of them were of the casement type, 6'x7', 5'x7', 6'x6', or 5'x6'. Possibly because they were the most exposed to public view, the outermost (E) and the innermost (A) rings had double-hung metal 5'x6' windows. All windows were equipped with metal venetian blinds. Because an undecorated entablature completely surrounds the fifth floor level of the building, there are no windows in the outside facade at that level. There are windows on the inward facing side of this (E) ring and on all of the other rings at the fifth floor level.

For appearances, and to provide space inside for air conditioning machinery and ducts, the architects put a sloping roof on the inner and outer rings and on the radial corridors. An early official description of the building, prepared by the Historical Branch of the War Department, described this adaptation.

> *The 960-foot-long roof-ridges of the outside ring presented a problem to the architects. If designed perfectly level, the roof of gray-green slate would have seemed to sag unless care was taken to avoid an optical illusion which has long been known. In meeting the same problem, the Greek designers of the Parthenon at Athens gave its roof-ridge a very slight arching curve. On three sides of The Pentagon the difficulty is solved in part by adding to the middle section of the facade parapets which break the line of the roof. To complete the solution, optical illusion has been matched very handily against optical illusion: a long row of recessed columns on each side tends to build up the middle section. Many people do not observe that this section of each of three facades, extending about one-half of its total length, projects some ten feet. A monotonous expanse of flat surface is avoided, and the center is still further strengthened. For the other two facades, one fronting north on the Mall and the other (adjacent) to the northeast, the same end is achieved by prominently projecting porticos which employ free-standing recessed columns.*

These two plain but attractive porticos, the River and Mall Entrances, projecting about 20 feet from the building, have a row of square columns and a broad sweep of steps. The River Entrance overlooks the scenic lagoon and Washington across the river. The 900-ft.-long stepped terrace, 450 ft. wide at its maximum, extends to the lagoon, where two monumental stairways on either side lead down to a landing dock, which until the late 1960s, was used by boats carrying military and civilian personnel between the Pentagon and Bolling Air Force Base down the river. The Mall Entrance enjoys the vista of a terrace measuring 600 ft. by 125 ft.; at its foot is a parade ground 600 ft. by 300 ft. The two entrances would become the usual entry for prominent visitors and often the scene of welcoming, farewell, and other ceremonies.

Construction progress on Section A, November 1941

Economy of movement was also facilitated by precise identification of offices. Each room is numbered according to floor, ring, nearest corridor, and specific office number. Thus room 3E881, the office of the secretary of defense, was on the third floor, ring E, off of corridor 8 (but could be reached from corridor 9 also), and its office number on the ring was 81. This system proved to be effective and has remained unchanged over the years, although some changes in office numbers have occurred as the result of alterations in space, particularly the division of bays into individual offices.

Movement of the many thousands of workers to and from and within the building required careful consideration by the planners. Two giant parking lots on opposite sides of the building (North and South Parking) provided space for 4,000 cars each on more than 54 acres of ground. To accommodate the large number of workers arriving and departing by bus and taxi, three 20-ft. lanes traversed the building from one end to the other at ground level.

From the bus platforms, 21 stairways provided access up to the Concourse, and from there six 30-ft.-wide ramps led to the interior of the building at three floor levels—second to fourth. Other ramps would connect main interior corridors, some to the fifth floor. The ramps, plus a number of escalators running as high as the fourth floor, permitted rapid direct movement of workers to their offices and to and from transportation. Elevators, of which there would be 13, would be chiefly for distribution of supplies and freight and consequently were large and unadorned, except for the private elevator of the highest ranking official in the building—first the secretary of war and later the secretary of defense. Disabled people would be permitted to use the freight elevators.

Arrangement of office space within the building stressed flexibility by leaving open most of the large bays—many of them 50 x 400 ft. or more—in the rings between corridors. This made possible the maximum use of space for the maximum number of workers and interfered least with heating and cooling the building. Private offices were provided for the most senior officials and additional separate work spaces were created by the use of movable partitions. Over the years most of the open bays gave way to separate enclosed offices, thus diminishing the population capacity of the building and placing a greater strain on the heating and cooling systems.

Schematic drawing, 1942

Another internal arrangement eventually had to be decided by the president himself. The location of the Pentagon in Virginia raised the question of racial segregation early in the construction. In March 1942 Groves inquired of Renshaw whether separate toilet facilities were being provided for whites and blacks as required by Virginia law. There arose also the matter of separate eating facilities, and consideration was given to placing a dining area for "colored people" in the basement. Although by this time the acquisition from Virginia of exclusive jurisdiction over the Pentagon military reservation left the federal government free to do as it pleased in such matters, the Engineer officers appeared disposed to opt for separate facilities. Moreover, Groves was either unaware of or ignored the president's Executive Order No. 8802 of 25 June 1941 which forbade discrimination because of "race, creed, color, or national origin" in the federal government and by federal contractors. This was the first official order by a president protecting Negro rights since the issuance of the Emancipation Proclamation by Abraham Lincoln on 1 January 1863.

Maj. Gen. Leslie R. Groves, 1944

The segregation issue in the Pentagon was probably resolved by President Roosevelt. According to Constance M. Green, author of *Washington, Capital City, 1879-1950*, "a story describing an inspection tour the President and Harry Hopkins made of the nearly completed Pentagon told of their astonishment at finding four huge washrooms placed along each of the five axes that connected the outer ring to the inmost on each floor of the building; upon inquiring the reason for such prodigality of lavatory space, the President was informed that non-discrimination required as many rooms marked 'Colored Men' and 'Colored Women' as 'White Men' and 'White Women'. The differentiating signs were never painted on the doors." Consideration of segregation of eating facilities in the building was also abandoned. Although Washington remained in many ways a segregated city, the federal government's actions beginning in 1941 led to the gradual lowering of the bars of racial discrimination.

Chart 3

Organization of the Army (The Marshall Reorganization)
9 March 1942

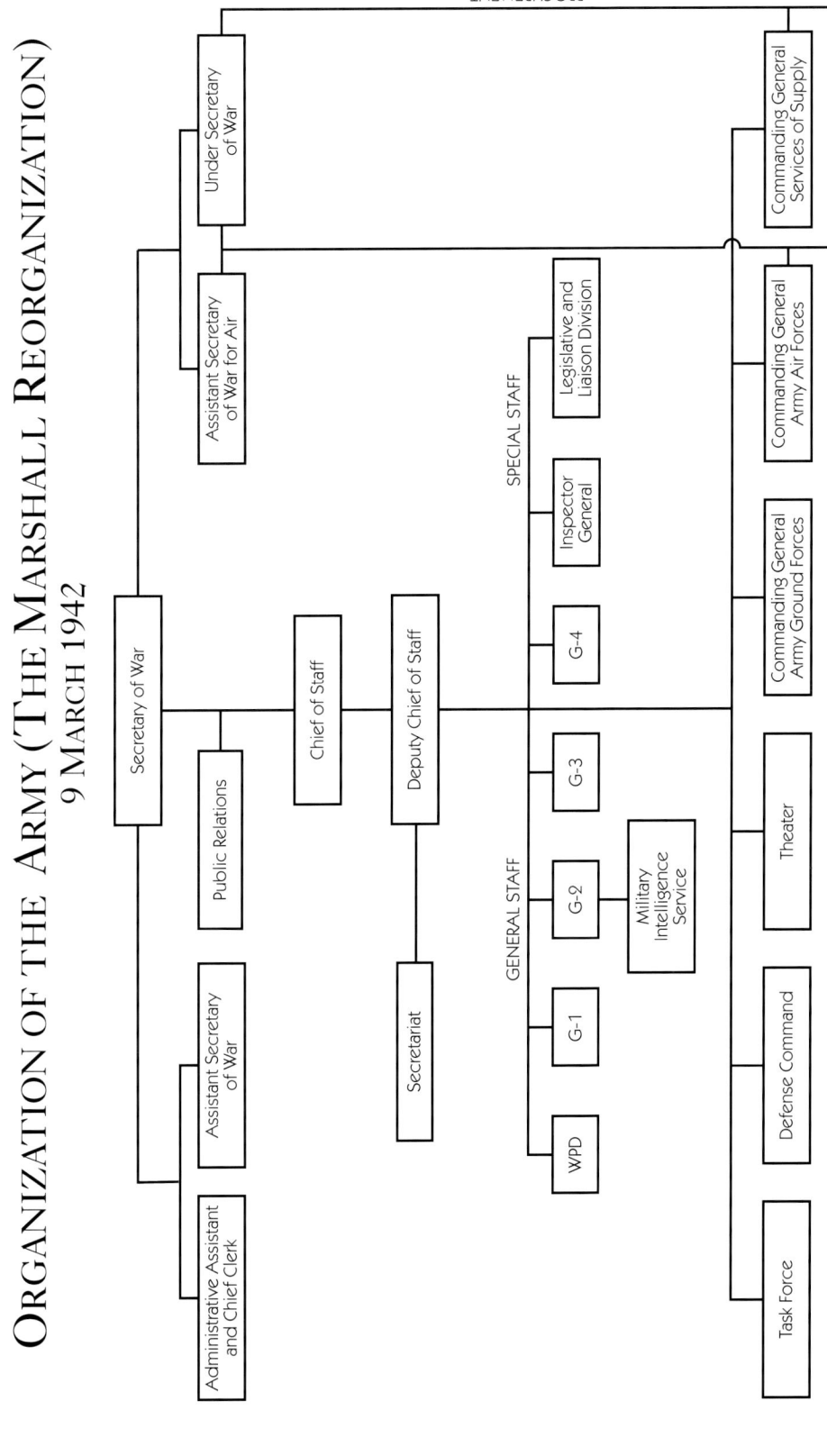

Source: War Department Circular 29, 2 March 1942

Outside the building loomed the formidable task of creating a complex road system to carry the heavy vehicular traffic in the vicinity of the building and across the Potomac.

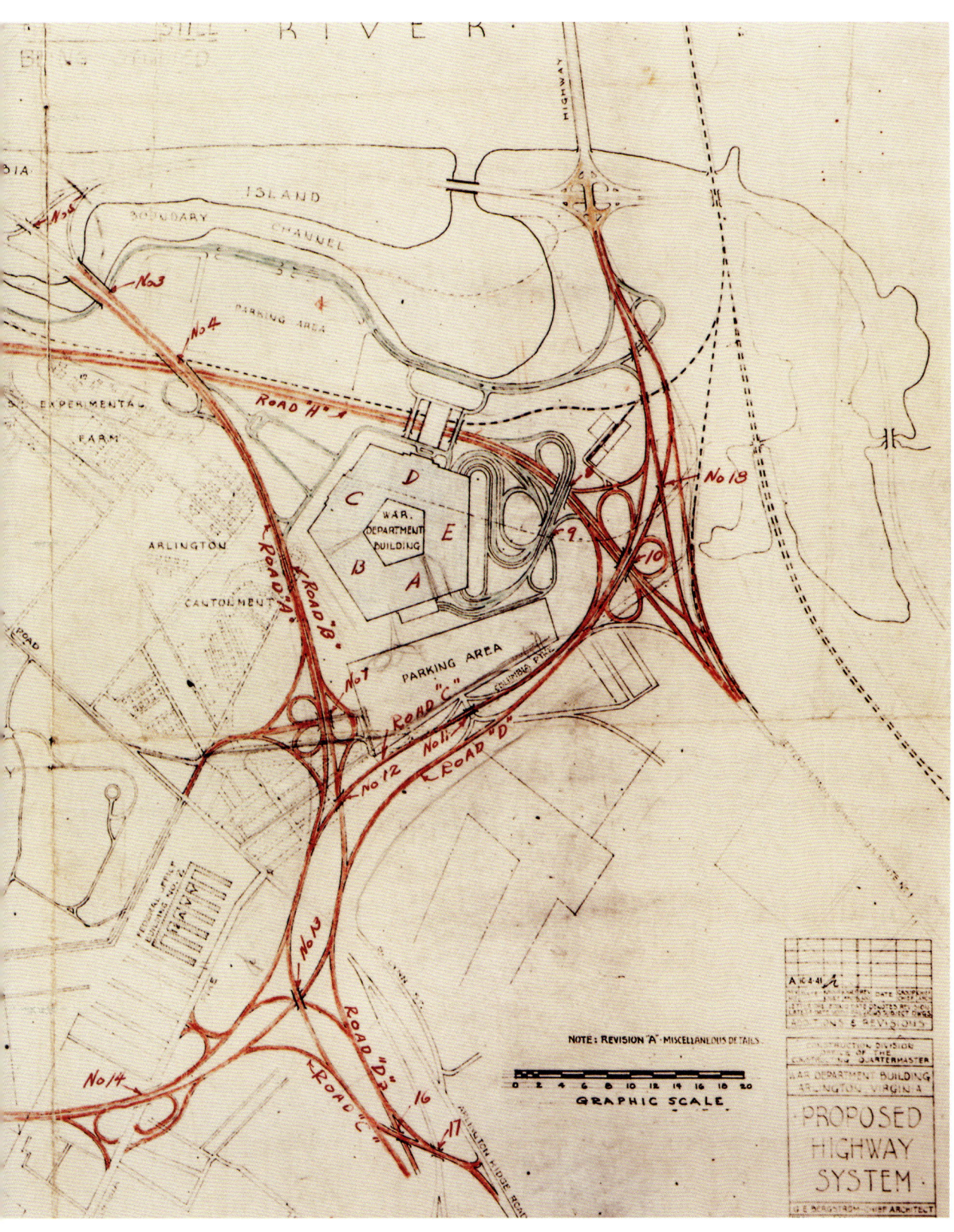

This construction was second only to the building itself in scope and cost. The highways constructed for the Pentagon turned out to be almost the same as originally advanced for the area by the National Capital Park and Planning Commission in 1934 and again in March 1941. It seems clear that traffic conditions on the Virginia side of the three Potomac River bridges required major improvements even before the Pentagon construction was authorized; the nearby National Airport had just been opened and the Navy Department's Navy Annex was under construction. The Pentagon's urgent need for the roads no doubt accelerated their completion. Otherwise the system would have been built over a much longer period of time.

The original authorization of $35 million for the Pentagon did not include any money for roads. The responsibility for road building lay with the Public Roads Administration (PRA) and the expectation was that it would provide the funds and oversee the construction of the system. Because of delays in legislation providing funds to the PRA and because the funds appropriated were not adequate to meet the agency's greatly enlarged building programs, the War Department found it necessary to advance funds for the road work. Eventually, by the end of 1943, the total cost of the highway system amounted to $17,686,300. The War Department paid about $7 million of this for acquisition of rights-of-way by the PRA, for construction work for the PRA, and for direct allotment to the agency for highway construction. The Corps of Engineers did not believe that these highway costs were properly chargeable to the cost of the building but accepted as proper outlays for access roads from the main highways to the parking areas and the building. The charges for "access roads, parking areas, and drainage outside building" amounted to $6,301,080.

The road system for the new building had to be able to handle very heavy traffic in cars and buses coming from several directions. In all, there were five routes for traffic from Virginia, Maryland, and the District of Columbia. The intricate network required 30 miles of new highway, ramps, 3 of the innovative cloverleaf exchanges, and 21 overpasses that permitted the elimination of grade crossings and traffic lights. In the early days (and perhaps since) it was a common experience for bus drivers and motorists to become confused and wander around the maze of roads, cloverleafs, and ramps for what must have seemed hours before finding their way to or from the building.

The architects and engineers were at pains to bring the building and its approaches into harmony with the general park development between the Potomac and the Arlington National Cemetery. Some 200,000 cu. yds. of top soil were used to create approximately 20 acres of lawn. Landscaping was kept simple, confined chiefly to grading and planting of grass, shrubs, and small trees. No large trees were planted. Formal planting of the center court and the terraces outside the Mall and River Entrances awaited the end of the war.

Considerations of landscaping also affected the siting and construction of auxiliary buildings needed to provide indispensable services for the Pentagon. The provision of utilities—heat, air conditioning, sewage treatment, water, and electricity—required major planning and construction efforts. The boiler plant, a substantial structure on a large site to provide heating and cooling for the Pentagon, met with objections from the Fine Arts Commission because of both its utilitarian appearance and its location. It was moved to a less prominent location and connected with the Pentagon by a 1,320 ft. tunnel. Similarly, the plant to treat the building's sewage and that of other facilities in the vicinity (principally the Navy Annex, then also under construction) had to be extensively screened by shrubbery to allay the Commission's displeasure at its appearance.

New road and overpasses, August 1942

There was no precedent for such a sewage plant, and much of the equipment had to be invented. It had to provide complete and effective sewage treatment because of the Pentagon's proximity to the Potomac River. The plant's array of tanks, filters, sludge dispensers, and sand drying beds, with a capacity of 3.2 million gallons per day, represented the state of the art in 1942. The decision to provide water and sewage capacity for other buildings in the vicinity also made it necessary to increase the size of these facilities, resulting in increased costs charged to Pentagon construction.

The utilities that made everything possible—water, electricity, and telephone service—had to come from the other side of the Potomac. Water came from Washington via a huge 30 in. concrete main across the Key Bridge and thence by steel pipes almost two miles down the Potomac shore to the building. This large demand necessitated additional filter capacity at the Dalecarlia Reservoir on the Washington bank of the river. To provide electricity, the Potomac Electric Power Company built a high voltage switching station near the building that served not only the Pentagon but also other buildings in the vicinity. The Buzzard's Point Generating Station in Washington provided the power via two submarine cables under the Potomac. For telephone service, 12 submarine cables were placed in 2,000-ft. trenches in the riverbed between Washington and the Pentagon.

Interior, heating and cooling plant, December 1942

Heating and cooling plant

Conception and Construction 69

*Construction progress,
December 1941*

Architects and draftsmen in Eastern Air Lines hangar

Section A progress, January 1942

Section B, basement to third floor, February 1942

View from roof of Navy Annex, March 1942

The telephone system was, of course, indispensable to the effective operation of the War Department staff in the building and, indeed, occupation could not begin until telephone service became available. The system installed in 1942 required 32,000 sq. ft. of space and had more than 200 employees and 125 switchboard positions. Heralded as the largest private branch telephone exchange in the world, it provided service not only for the Pentagon but for the other War Department buildings in the Washington area. It was one of the earliest and presumably the largest automatic direct dialing system, serving tens of thousands of War Department phones.

Telephone switchboard

The early occupants apparently performed effectively amid the chaos of construction and the continual shifting of offices while the building was being constructed around them. There were many complaints about inadequate transportation and parking, cafeteria food and service, and problems with water, electricity, and other utilities. There were even suggestions from employees who complained about transportation problems that overnight sleeping accommodations be provided on the fourth and fifth floors. All of these complaints had validity, but such troubles had to be accepted as normal under the extraordinary circumstances of the building's construction and sequential occupancy.

Center Court construction, May 1942

River E
Lagoon

The early occupants apparently performed effectively amid the chaos of construction and the continual shifting of offices while the building was being constructed around them. There were many complaints about inadequate transportation and parking, cafeteria food and service, and problems with water, electricity, and other utilities. There were even suggestions from employees who complained about transportation problems that overnight sleeping accommodations be provided on the fourth and fifth floors. All of these complaints had validity, but such troubles had to be accepted as normal under the extraordinary circumstances of the building's construction and sequential occupancy.

Center Court construction, May 1942

Two anecdotes of the construction period in 1942-43 attest to the hectic conditions that existed at the time. A timekeeper who worked in an engineer's "shack" at the construction site came to work one morning but couldn't find the building. During the night, a giant bulldozer had moved it to another site. One near-victim of a cave-in described how she and fellow office workers had to jump over their desks to escape fresh cement that poured down like molten lava from a collapsed wall behind them. Not all of the hazards of wartime were confined to the battlefield.

Four sections in view, June 1942

The decision to complete the fifth floor came in July 1942 when Somervell, in response to the strong recommendation of Assistant Secretary McCloy, directed that the addition "be added to the three interior rings . . . to increase the utility of the Pentagon Building." This required removal of some fourth floor roofing and coping that had already been installed, thereby increasing costs. Previously, the fifth floor had been confined to the two outer rings. The change permitted the addition of 350,000 sq. ft. of office space and the accommodation of a greater building population. It also created additional storage space. Also in July, it was decided to provide heating and ventilation for the basement, originally intended for dead storage but now required for office space.

From the beginning, the highest levels of the War Department had adamantly opposed the construction of an athletic facility in the building, fearing adverse congressional and public reaction. At this time they yielded to the extent of permitting provision of basic locker and shower facilities in an undeveloped area of the basement under the terraces. Later, after the war, at the instigation of then Chief of Staff Dwight D. Eisenhower, a variety of facilities, including a gymnasium and a swimming pool, were added.

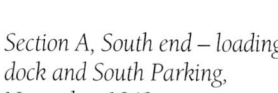

Section A, South end – loading dock and South Parking, November 1942

An investigation of the building's progress conducted by the Bureau of the Budget in August 1942 criticized some aspects of the project, particularly cost and architecture, but, uncharacteristically for such reports, it had high praise for the leadership of the undertaking. "In order to have made the progress that has obtained unmistakably indicates that the men responsible for this project were able and fearless constructors possessed of a large fund of amicability and common sense." The report praised "the supreme command of the prime contractors held by Mr. John McShain" as "largely responsible for the procurement and scheduling of the vast numbers and quantities of labor and material, as well as the coordination of the work with their other organizations."

A brief survey entitled "Planning The Pentagon Building," probably prepared by Witmer in October 1942, paid special tribute to Renshaw. "In last analysis, the District Engineer, Lieut. Colonel Renshaw, was responsible for the early completion of the building. He alone could represent the War Department, make decisions in the interest of speeding the work and direct the design office, the builder and the inspection force to the end that the work should be accomplished as speedily as possible. The shortness of time from commencement of building to completion is quite as much due to his driving force and his determination to remove causes of hindrance as the cooperation and efforts of all parties engaged in the work." Perhaps the most compelling proof of Renshaw's effectiveness was that he satisfied two such hard drivers as Somervell and Groves, who would not have hesitated a moment to relieve him had he failed to deliver.

Col. Clarence Renshaw, 1946

The labor force performed exceptionally well, particularly after Pearl Harbor, under difficult and often dangerous circumstances. Carpenters were plentiful but there were shortages in other trades—especially plumbers, sheet metal workers, and steamfitters. According to the Bureau of the Budget report at the end of August 1942, when the construction was 80 percent completed: "Although the work was well staffed no loafing to speak of was observed on the several inspection trips around the project. It is the rule here that if a man is found loafing without cause, he is dismissed and his name is placed on a list that bars his reemployment on the work thereafter." Moreover, "no unusual difficulties were experienced with the unions" which "were satisfied with their treatment." Workmen received meals at cafeterias at cost.

The Pentagon exacted a toll from its creators. The early months of construction in 1941 were marred by a high accident rate, four times the rate for Army construction as a whole. By December there had been 40 accidents, including one fatality. Seven more deaths occurred before the end of August 1942, six of them in accidents and one from heat exhaustion. At the instigation of Groves and Renshaw, the chief contractor, McShain, employed full-time safety engineers, but this did not result in a measurable decline in the accident rate. It seemed that accidents were an unavoidable consequence of such a breakneck speed of construction. Another victim of the hectic pace was Luther Leisenring, who was carried out of his Construction Division office "on a slab" after a heart attack. He returned later as a consultant.

Preparing the tunnels, November 1942

It is probable that the building would have been ready closer to the date set for its completion—15 November 1942, only 14 months after groundbreaking—but for the troubles that beset it during construction. While most of these troubles were common to the experience of other large building ventures, there were more of them, a reflection of the magnitude of the project. Foremost among the causes of delay was the July 1942 decision to add a fifth floor. The building was complete on 15 November except for the fifth floor. Of serious import also were the difficulty of the site and the weather. Working throughout the winter months presented major problems in maintaining the pace of construction. In some measure this was met by the continual addition of workers—in the 6 or 7 months after Pearl Harbor more than 10,000 joined the 4,000 who were on the job on 7 December 1941. A variety of minor labor problems—strikes, jurisdictional disputes between unions and over non-union workers, complaints about working hours and conditions, and periodical shortages of workers in special skills—

River Entrance, Terrace and Lagoon, November 1942

had some effect on construction progress. Fortunately, none of these generally brief incidents provoked prolonged work stoppages. Other causes of delay included fires, a burst water main that resulted in flooding, and transportation and parking difficulties that resulted in the loss of many work hours. And frequent differences between architects and builders over drawings and specifications did not help speed the work.

During the whole period of construction, and for some time thereafter, the Pentagon continued to be an object of disapproval and disparagement.* The press in particular appeared to have a strong dislike for this intruder on the local scene. The *Washington Post* told its readers that "Washington has many reasons to regret the construction of the gigantic War Department Building just off the chief approaches of the city from the south." The *Washington Evening Star* "doubted if Congress would have approved the building" had the actual costs been known originally. Two other local papers, the *Times-Herald* and the *Daily News*, seemed to relish highlighting negative aspects of the building's construction and occupation. The magazine *U.S. News* wrote: "One instinctively wonders what use will be found for a building of such gargantuan proportions after the war is succeeded by the inevitable disarmament pact. Perhaps the entire U.S. Army will be housed in it." *Newsweek* referred to the building as a "simple penitentiary-like structure." Bemusement with the sheer size of the building and its large population gave rise to anecdotes and stories that provided the stuff of an ever-expanding lore about the Pentagon.

* Many of the great federal government buildings in Washington had occasioned prolonged controversy, chiefly over their size, architectural appeal, cost, and suitability. The first building of consequence, the White House, was the object of much debate over its size, shape, and style. It was generally accepted as a successful structure after its completion in 1801 and remained the largest house in the country for much of the century. The Pension Building, erected in the 1880s by the Army, stirred a great deal of comment, much of it derisive, during its construction and after. The Commanding General of the Army, Philip H. Sheridan, loathed the building; he said that the worst thing about it "was that it was fireproof." The War Department's home for 60 years, the State, War, and Navy Building, now renamed the Old Executive Office Building, for many years after its completion in 1888 had its detractors. Mark Twain called it "the ugliest building in America," and Herbert Hoover found it "an architectural absurdity." But it survived these assaults and is one of the great landmarks of the nation's capital. Among twentieth century buildings, none have attracted more sustained and derogatory criticism than the massive Rayburn Office Building and the Federal Bureau of Investigation Building. In terms of architectural acceptance, the Pentagon has fared much better than either of these more recent buildings.

The official completion date for construction of the Pentagon was 15 January 1943. When the building began to come into use at the end of April 1942 it was thought desirable to give it a name that would distinguish it from the New War Department Building in Washington. In May 1942, the department announced that this newest War Department building would be known as the Pentagon; it officially confirmed the name on 19 February 1943. No dedication ceremony was held because of the pressures of wartime. Initially greeted with much humor, skepticism, and even derision, the Pentagon eventually became not only an enduring architectural success but a global symbol of American power and prestige.

High aerial view

Aerial view, Mall Entrance and Center Court

Part II
Pentagon Profiles

River Entrance in the spring, 1990

94 Pentagon Profiles

Many aspects of the Pentagon, as a functioning building over the years, invite attention and are deserving of commentary. Among the more significant ones treated in the pages following are architecture, cost, changes in the configuration and utilization of the building, the inhabitants, the National Military Command System, and impact on the environment. Additional detailed information about the building and its occupants is presented in appendixes.

Architecture

The great size of the Pentagon has tended to overshadow, in the public eye, the building's architectural style. That style, known as "Stripped Classicism," was a synthesis of classical and modern style characteristic of many federal buildings designed between the 1930s and the 1950s. Although the design and ornamentation are in the classic style, they have been simplified, retaining such decorative elements of the classical mode as columns and moldings, but in an understated manner. The buildings also retained traditional features such as symmetry of design and exterior decorative elements layered from top to bottom.

The Pentagon is the largest and most prominent example of the stripped classical architectural style. Other government structures of this style in Washington built during the same period are the Federal Reserve Building, the Department of Interior Building, the New War Department Building (incorporated in the State Department Building), and the Main Terminal at Washington National Airport.

The building presents a clean delineation of top, middle, and bottom. The entablature* around the building is greater over the central colonnades of the five outer facades. A cornice of ornamental molding wraps around the entire building, separating the entablature from the middle level of the facades, which consist of three rows of evenly-spaced windows around the building. These are symmetrical except when interrupted by colonnades. A central focus in each facade is achieved by a 140-ft. colonnade placed in the middle, each containing 16 rectangular columns 36 ft. high.

* An entablature is an architecturally treated wall that rests on the capitals of the columns and supports the pediment or roof plate. In ascending order it consists of the architrave, the frieze, and the cornice.

Far left, Mall Entrance
Below, River Entrance and Lagoon

Architectural evaluations of the Pentagon have become more positive with the passage of time and changes in architectural style. An early commentary appeared in the *Architectural Forum* in January 1943. "About the building's exterior," it pronounced, "the less said the better: in essence it is the official Washington front, stretched thin to cover 4,600 running feet of facade. It is presented here because a building so enormous takes on a quality which depends not on the 'architecture' but on its size and the problems that go with it." The critique sensed the environmental impact of such large-scale construction. "For miles around the results of building the Pentagon are visible: the reclaimed slums, the broad roads, and the new, integrated approaches to the capital. Perhaps the greatest lesson of the Pentagon is here: as building approaches the scale technically feasible, the distinction between architecture and city planning vanishes. Despite its shortcomings, the Pentagon gives a real foretaste of the future."

A more favorable official appreciation in 1945, before the end of the war, noted that the building was "planned for efficiency, not beauty," that it was the least imitative of Washington public buildings, and that it had a "quiet dignity." Moreover, the building's effect was "Hellenic in its simplicity. . . modern in its lack of curves, its rigid formality, and its vastness." "Utility determined design" in a building that was completely functional. "Its massive, fortress-like outline suggests at once its multiple function."

In an article in January 1968, on the twenty-fifth anniversary of the Pentagon, the architectural critic of the *New York Times*, Ada Louise Huxtable, spoke a kind, if grudging, word: "Called too big, too barren, and too expensive when it was completed for $83 million in 1943, the Pentagon is a thriving, functional success in 1968." On the occasion of the building's fortieth anniversary in 1983, the architectural critic of the *Washington Post*, Benjamin Forgey, emphasized its positive features.

> *Up close, the building seems much less awesome than it should, given its actual size. It is in outline, a respectful, traditional Washington building: low, divided into the traditional base, middle and top, symmetrical, punctuated by projecting colonnaded pavilions on each facade to help break plane and mass—in other words, in its limited way a crisp piece of work.*
>
> *The Pentagon, in short, was a no-nonsense building. . . .*
>
> *Spurred by the necessities of war, the government was building the kind of thoroughly planned environment modern architects had so far been able only to write and dream about, and architects and planners world-wide were impressed. Much has been said about the Pentagon's labyrinthine qualities, but in fact the building is extremely rational, and extremely modernist, in plan. As a sort of comprehensive pedestrian city in miniature, it was extremely advanced for its time, a precursor of the kind of megastructure and mega-environment (e.g., the Hancock Building in Chicago) that private industry would not begin building for decades. The best thing about the Pentagon in this respect is that it is horizontal not vertical: city planners, corporate clients, and architects still might ponder the usefulness of that lesson.*
>
> *. . .The Pentagon today can hardly help but be a mind numbing place. Fortunately it is rather easy on the eyes.*

The historical and architectural merit of the Pentagon was recognized when it was placed on the National Register of Historic Places in 1989. In the years following its completion in 1943, the Pentagon interior and surroundings underwent considerable change, including construction of additional parking areas and a heliport and alterations in the road system. But the exterior remained as was and provided the basis for the nomination to the historic register. Appropriately, the nomination cited five elements of the building as qualifying factors:

1. The five outer facades
2. The Central Courtyard and the surrounding facade
3. The terrace fronting the Mall Entrance
4. The terrace fronting the River Entrance
5. The distinctive five-sided shape

The designated area comprised a total of 41 acres.

River Entrance ceremony

The Pentagon was designed and constructed as a utilitarian building. The persistent criticisms of almost every aspect of the building—site, size, materials, facilities, equipment, and, of course, cost—caused the War Department hierarchy most concerned with the construction of the building—McCloy, Marshall, and Somervell—to insist on strong measures to ensure austerity in both the exterior and interior designs. There were no ostentatious ornamentations and no superfluous architectural features, unless one chooses to regard columns and porticos as such. In a letter to Representative Woodrum in October 1942 Somervell emphasized that there were "no unnecessary architectural features, such as marble halls, fountains, statuary, and the like." Nor was there time to consider and plan the kinds of exterior and interior refinements found in other federal buildings such as the Department of Justice, the Supreme Court, and the National Archives, all built during the 1930s. These could be designed and constructed at a relatively leisurely pace, unlike the Pentagon. The strong pressures to keep the Pentagon simple and unadorned derived from presidential and congressional concern about the cost and eventual use of the building for other purposes after the war, from the use of substitute materials, and from press and public criticism of the project in general.

Center Court at lunchtime, c. 1950

102 Pentagon Profiles

*Program in Center Court
At table General Thomas T. Handy,
General Carl A. Spaatz, and
General Dwight D. Eisenhower, 1946*

Except for the suites of the highest ranking civilian and military officials, the offices were stark in their simplicity and bareness. Amenities were originally confined to eating places—cafeterias and snack bars—but others, including an athletic facility and shopping facilities on the Concourse, were added later. Landscaping was kept simple, limited to grading and planting of grass, shrubs, and small trees. The lagoon below the River Entrance, made possible by the extensive excavation of large amounts of earth used for road and parking area fill, had more than a landscaping purpose. It made possible the raising of roads and parking areas above flood level, thus obviating the need for a levee and converting 100 acres of marginal land into 70 acres of usable land.

Original cafeteria, 1942

The Pentagon has unity, oneness. It hangs together and it works. It commands attention not because of its beauty—it is not a visual delight—but because of its size and its function. The mixture of pragmatic and aesthetic is obviously weighted on the side of the former. Even before its completion the building was described unfavorably and often disdainfully as gigantic, gargantuan, massive, and fortress-like. Some called it a monstrosity. And yet one is not overwhelmed by the building, certainly not at a distance and not even close up. The impression is one of solidity rather than great mass—it is compact in spite of its size.

Cafeteria, 1991

Center Court, 1992

Inevitably, the Pentagon invited comparison, chiefly statistical, with other great structures, both historic and contemporary. Such comparisons invariably recited that five U.S. Capitol Buildings, with wings, could be accommodated within the new building, that it had three times the floor space of the Empire State Building, and that it was 50 percent larger than the Merchandise Mart in Chicago. According to one source, "The great Pyramid of Cheops could be dropped there with room left for the Sphinx!" The Pentagon has one-and-a-half times the space of the Sears Tower in Chicago, a more recent addition to the architectural scene. Another late entrant to the competition for "biggest building," the World Trade Center in New York, completed in 1973, has more than nine million square feet of floor space, but it consists of two twin towers.

The creation of an attractive if not imposing setting, in spite of the serious physical constraints of a troublesomely wet, uneven, and unattractive site, in a way made a silk purse out of a sow's ear. The building is distinct from its surroundings yet an integral part of a harmonious whole of landscape—trees, shrubs, lawn, lagoon, walks, roads, and yes, parking areas. The requirement for auxiliary utility buildings and huge parking areas covering many acres diminished opportunities for landscaping to make the site yet more attractive. Still, much of the building's appeal lies in such strong points as the main entrances and their handsome terraces and the showpiece center court. This good land use derived from a sound fundamental concept that incorporated a sensitive approach to the environment.

The view of the Pentagon from elevated roads that bypass the building offers a better sense of proportion and setting than a view from site level. Indeed, the proportions are satisfying. Because the height and length are an excellent match the impact of the building's size is reduced. Had the building been lower—the original planned three stories—it is likely that the perspective would be less in accord with its surroundings and less pleasing. Perhaps by chance as much as by design, the five-story height appears to have provided the optimum proportion for the sweeping structure.

Five Capitol Buildings inside the Pentagon (with permission of Popular Mechanics)

The virtues of the building far exceed its flaws. It gives an impression of permanence, coherence, and consistency—strong, simple, and even appealing. It is spacious and conveys a sense of contained stability and dignity. The epic scale of the structure makes for a powerful physical presence and marks it as obviously a building of public importance and a landmark. It is plain, perhaps even severe, but it is not forbidding, nor is it completely unadorned—the severity is much relieved by the columns, projecting porticoes with columns, parapets, and plazas and terraces. This helps create a balanced composition which lends visual order and harmony. It is true that there are no subtleties about the building, but it has quality and dignity and achieves a measure of style with a minimum of effort. Moreover, this colossus has met the test of architectural responsibility—it has accomplished its purpose admirably. Within the governing constraints of time, site, size, and cost it is difficult to imagine that a building any more attractive or utilitarian than the Pentagon could have been built.

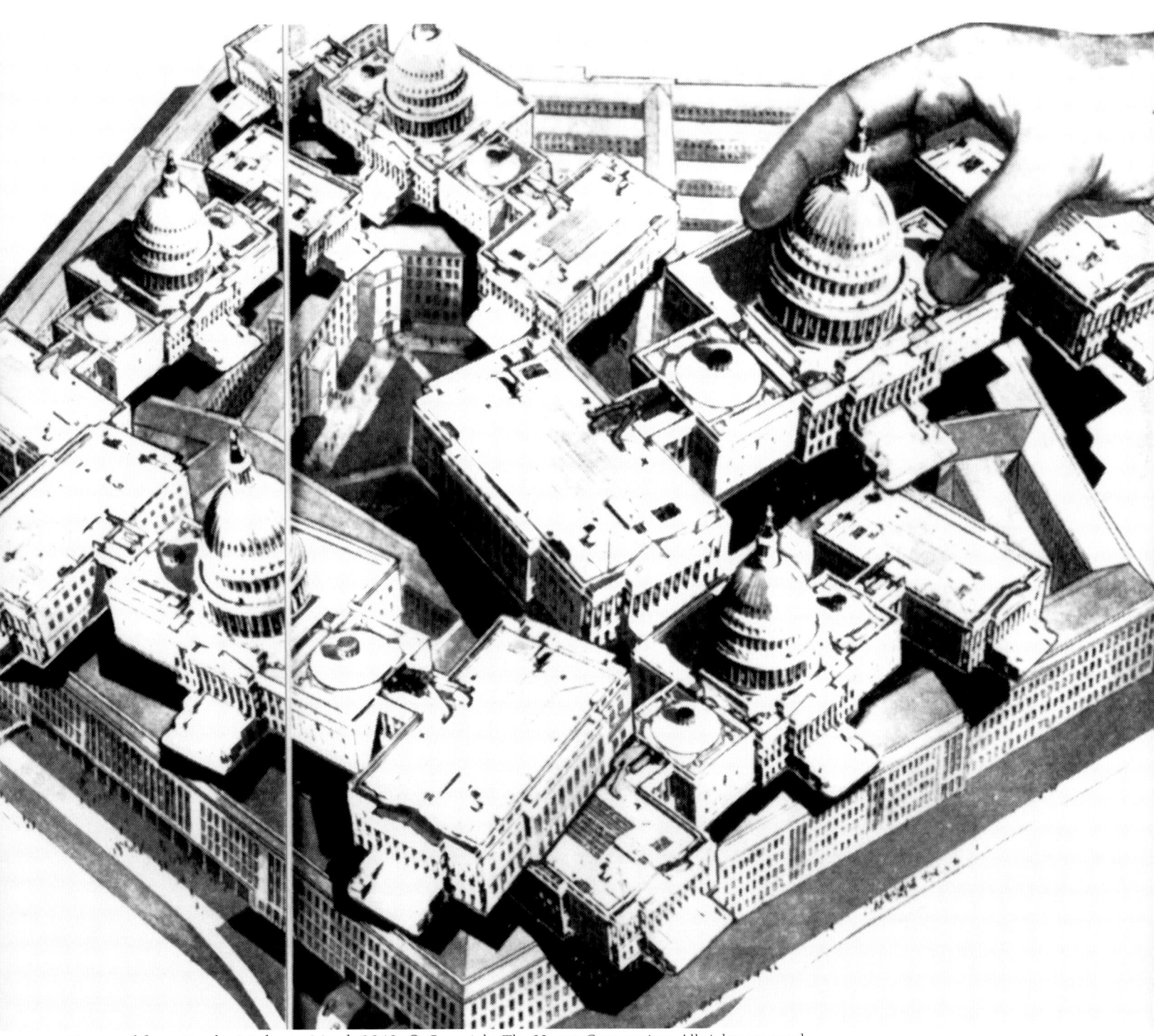

Reprinted from *Popular Mechanics* March 1943. © Copyright The Hearst Corporation. All rights reserved.

Cost

As might have been expected because of its size and prominence, the cost of the Pentagon was an issue from the very beginning. In July 1941 Somervell had given the House Appropriations Committee a construction estimate of $35 million for the original Arlington Farms site, exclusive of parking. In August, with reference to the relocation to the Quartermaster depot site, he informed a Senate committee that it was "impossible . . . to give . . . any accurate figure at the southern site." He added that there would be increased costs because of expensive grading and foundation requirements and additional roads.

Much of Washington could watch the building rising and spreading on the Virginia side of the Potomac. The extensive and continual attention that the project excited prompted strong expressions of concern about the projected costs from both members of Congress and the press. The most virulent and prolonged attacks had a strong political tinge, especially during election years—1942 and 1944. The Roosevelt Administration, General Somervell, and the Corps of Engineers served as whipping boys for the critics. In Congress, the foremost critic was Rep. Albert J. Engel (Mich.) who frequently attacked Somervell and the War Department over a period of three years, alleging irregularities and excessive costs in the whole Army construction program. The Pentagon received particular attention from Engel since it was under his very nose in Washington. By October 1942, when Engel was charging that the building would cost $70 million, twice the original estimate of $35 million, Washington newspapers were joining him in his attacks. The *Washington Post* in an editorial spoke of "lavish expenditure," "unwarranted disregard of congressional intent," and "a very costly experiment." The *Washington Evening Star* found "the costs as now revealed are certainly staggering." It "doubted if Congress would have approved the building, had these costs been known then." The War Department, from Secretary Stimson and Under Secretary Patterson down to the Construction Division of the Corps of Engineers, found itself on the defensive and had to prepare frequent responses to congressional inquiries about costs.

Earlier, it had become clear to the Corps of Engineers that the extensive changes in the Pentagon's construction would increase the cost substantially. April 1942 estimates added $14.25 million for changes resulting chiefly from the shift in location ($7.45 million), increase in load bearing capacity ($2 million), additional utility construction ($1.45 million), and accelerated construction ($2.47 million). On 7 May Somervell notified the Appropriations Committees of both houses of Congress of the increased costs, explained the causes, and asserted that the additional funds could be provided from other unexpended balances of War Department construction projects. The committees accepted the explanation and took no further action. Once again, in October, Somervell had to reply to charges from Engel that he had concealed the full cost of the building from Congress and had spent more money than had been appropriated. The tide of public and congressional support of the military and its requirements was running strong at this early critical period of the war, and there was not yet much disposition to question military requests for funds.

Left, River Entrance, 1990

*File room of the
Adjutant General's Office*

Possible Alternative Uses

Any notions that the Pentagon might eventually be converted to other uses were quickly dispelled. Rumors and gossip had conjectured that it would be used one day as a hospital, an archives repository, or an educational institution, but none of these uses ever received serious consideration.

Before and during construction President Roosevelt and others speculated vaguely that it might be used as a records repository after the war. However, the unstable and threatening postwar world required that the United States maintain a military establishment many times larger than ever before in peacetime, which in turn required the retention of large military headquarters organizations in Washington. Thus the Pentagon remained the nerve center of the War Department, albeit with a somewhat diminished population. At the same time, the building still could not accommodate the smaller departmental work force, making necessary the continued use of other buildings, principally the temporary building (T-7) at Gravelly Point next to the National Airport, temporary buildings next to Fort McNair, and part of the Munitions Building.

It was estimated in 1947 that about 80 percent of the War Department staff was under the Pentagon roof, but this may have been too high since there were Army field establishments elsewhere in the vicinity that directly supported the departmental staff.

Chart 4

OFFICE OF THE SECRETARY OF DEFENSE
15 SEPTEMBER 1948

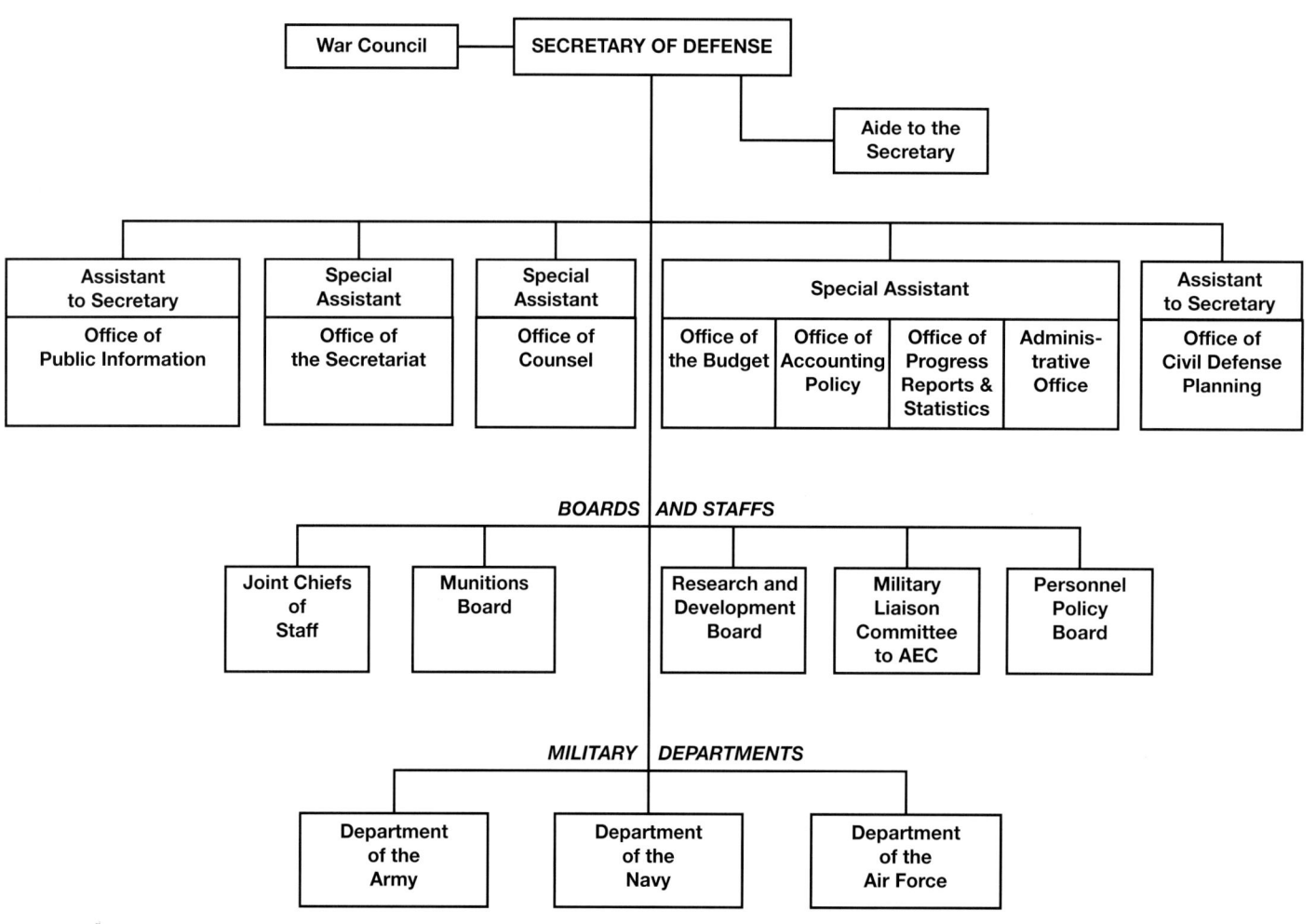

Structural Changes

Major structural changes that occurred within the building during its first half century resulted from pressure to provide more usable space and improved security. Fortunately, the flexibility of the interior design permitted easy and rapid adjustments in office space. The steady process of partitioning the open bays into separate offices had the effect of reducing overall office space. The movement into the building of additional agencies with high-ranking officials—chiefly the Navy Department and Joint Chiefs of Staff (JCS)—and the establishment of the separate Air Force created a demand for large suites of offices occupied by smaller numbers of people. This demand for generous space for higher officials continued as new positions came into being as a result of congressional or executive actions. The Office of the Secretary of Defense went from three to nine assistant secretaries in 1953, and more were added later. In 1978 two undersecretaries were added. Other high level offices were established at or near the assistant secretary level without the title of assistant secretary. The Joint Chiefs of Staff, initially limited to 100 officers, grew in increments to more than 400, plus hundreds of additional military and civilian personnel. The military departments added assistant secretaries and other high level officials, while the military staffs also added more high-ranking officers.

Open bay "Busy Bees"

To meet the demands for space for new and expanded functions, it was necessary periodically to move many offices out of the Pentagon to other parts of the Washington area. The search for additional room within the building led to the enclosure of previously open areas other than the office bays used chiefly for services and storage. They included spaces at the apex junctures of corridors with the inner or A ring, and on the ramps from this ring. Four of the original six cafeterias were made into office space, as was a substantial space on the third floor previously used for a bank relocated to the Concourse. Finishing off some of the roughed-in storage areas on the fifth floor provided additional space. These had not originally been intended for office use because they were in the windowless outside face of the outer ring.

Outside the building, on the north side, a helicopter pad constructed in 1955 was originally for the rapid evacuation of top civilian and military leaders in emergencies. Subsequently, it was used by all of the military services for official transportation to and from the building. The Army operated the 100 x 100 ft. concrete pad, handling hundreds of flights per month. A control tower was added in April 1959.

The Pentagon helicopter pad

View of Concourse

POW/MIA Corridor, 1990

Dedicated Corridors

The War Department leaders—particularly McCloy and Somervell—kept faith with Congress, adhering to their promise of no frills and adornments in the Pentagon interior. Throughout World War II and for some years afterward the halls remained *Spartan*—stark and unadorned. Gradually, the Office of the Secretary of Defense and the military departments decorated rings and corridors in their separate areas and in common areas in the A ring. Most of these dedicated corridors were on the second, third, and fourth floors, where the most important offices were located.

At the behest of Secretary of Defense Donald H. Rumsfeld in 1976, OSD undertook an expanded program of decoration in corridors, halls, and alcoves. The most prominent of these were a commander in chief corridor that displayed photographic portraits of all of the presidents; a bicentennial exhibit celebrating the anniversary of the Declaration of Independence; the Flag Corridor, exhibiting state flags and the various U.S. flags of the past 200 years; a corridor displaying the flags of the NATO nations; and a Hall of Heroes (holders of the Medal of Honor). Other OSD corridors included a display of portrait paintings of the secretaries of defense, an Eisenhower Corridor in the vicinity of the office of the secretary of defense, a military women's corridor, and a prisoner of war alcove.

The E Ring, Eisenhower Corridor

Hall of Heroes, 1990

View of NATO Corridor, 1990

The military departments and the Joint Chiefs of Staff have also established corridors to honor their leaders and heroes. Thus, portrait corridors honor the long lines of secretaries of the Army, secretaries of the Navy, chiefs of staff of the Army and Air Force, chiefs of naval operations, commandants of the Marine Corps, and the Joint Chiefs of Staff. Corridors are dedicated to General George C. Marshall, General Douglas A. MacArthur, General Henry H. Arnold, and General Omar Bradley—all five-star generals. In all, there are more than two dozen of these special corridors and areas. About a dozen corridors are included in the Pentagon Tour (75 minutes), open to the public since 1976. Other permanent exhibits on a smaller scale occur throughout the building, adding to its decor while imparting a sense of history and heritage.

Corridor of World War II paintings

TO FIRST FLOOR
TO NORTH PARKING
0417
0417
CUSHMAN

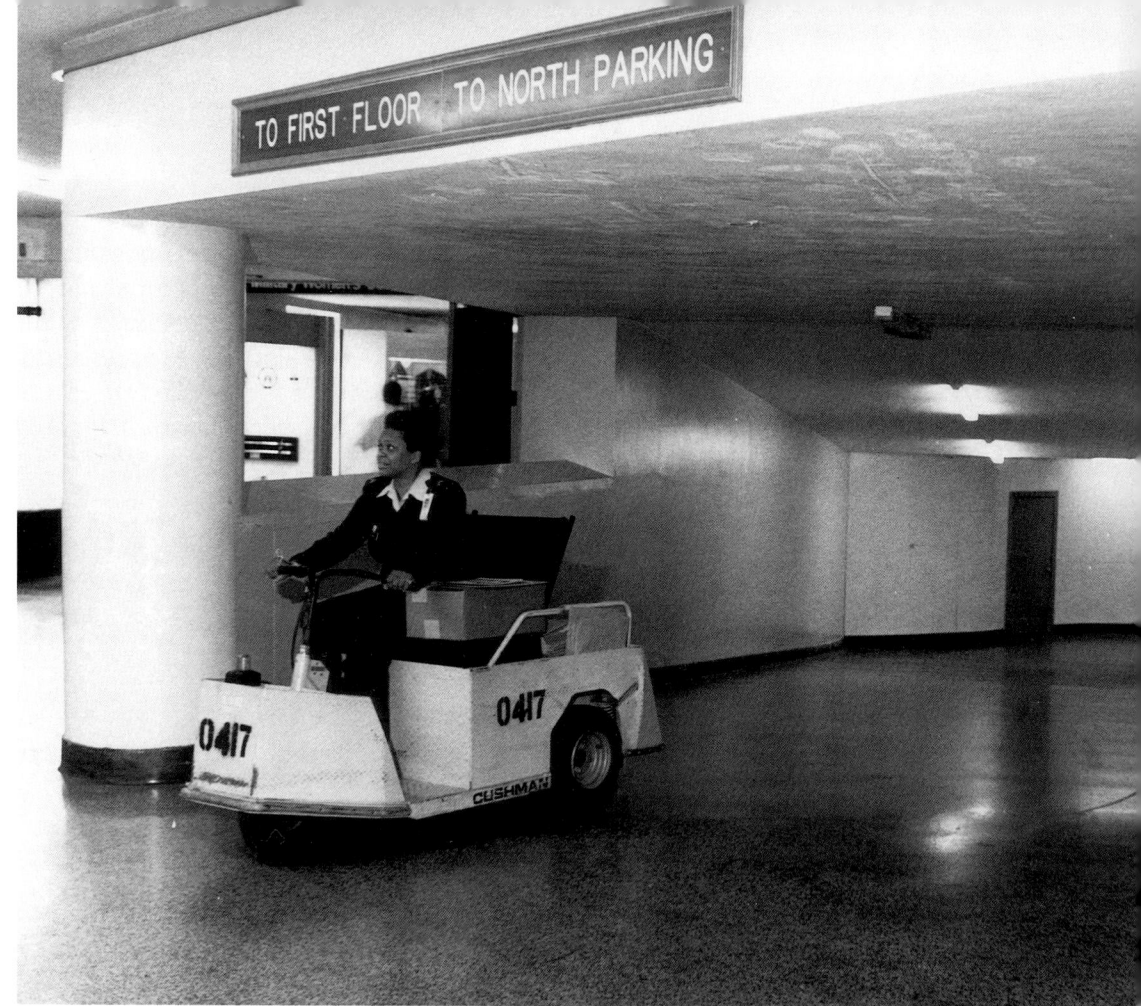

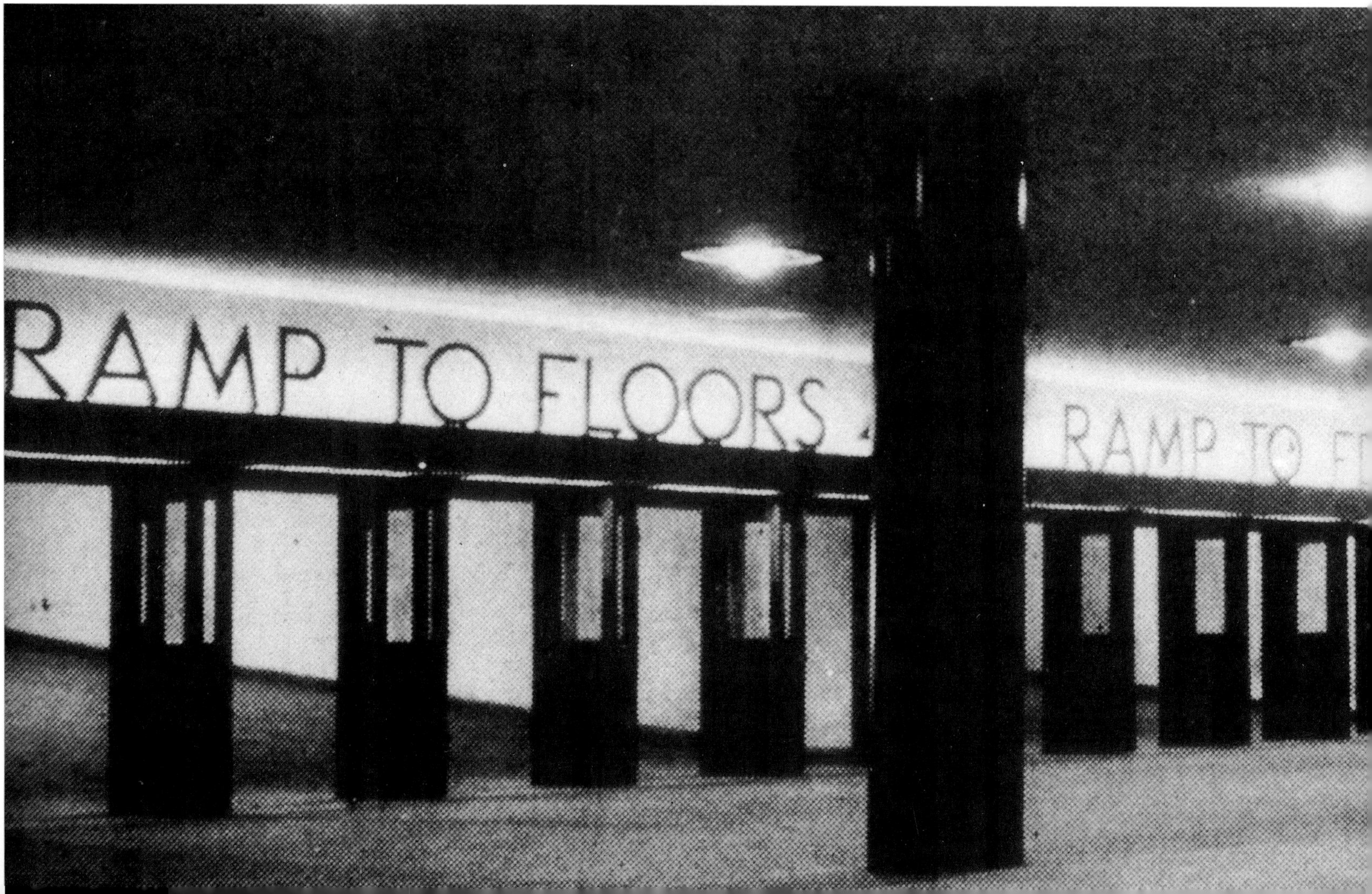
RAMP TO FLOORS

Inside Vehicles

A phenomenon that has affected the everyday work of the building and its physical structure as well has been the great increase in the number of vehicles employed within the building. Over the years the wide corridors have lent themselves to the use of a variety of vehicles for many purposes. In the early years pneumatic tubes were used for the movement of mail within the building, but these were succeeded by mounted messengers. The earlier bicycle-type vehicles, of which there were still many in the 1960s, gave way to vehicles powered by electric or gasoline motors. The vehicles grew larger and more numerous as functions became more mechanized. Trash collection came to be performed by operation of huge gondola-type vehicles pulled by tractor-type prime movers. Inevitably, this plethora of vehicles caused much physical damage in the building, gouging holes in walls and demolishing corridor corners, even those protected by heavy metal plates. Occasionally pedestrians suffered injuries when struck by vehicles. Among the victims was Secretary of the Air Force Eugene Zuckert (1961-65), run down at an intersection near his office. Traffic and safety regulations helped mitigate accidents and damage, but the physical damage proved difficult to eliminate. As in the larger traffic world outside, there was a price to pay for the convenience of mechanization. Renovation plans envisage eliminating all self-propelled vehicles from the building and returning to bicycle-type vehicles and handcarts.

Concourse construction, 1942

Transportation

Transporting 25,000 to 30,000 people plus hundreds, perhaps thousands of visitors to the Pentagon daily from a radius of 75 miles has required use of an effective combination of public and private vehicles. Commuters come from Baltimore, some 40-45 miles away; from Fredericksburg, Va., more than 50 miles away; and some from even more distant points. People have used trains, buses, cars, motorcycles, bicycles, and eventually a subway system. Pedestrians have remained few and no doubt weary.

Judging from the constantly overflowing parking lots, which accommodate some 10,000 vehicles, a growing number of Pentagon workers arrive by private motor vehicle—car, van, truck, jeep. Increasingly these carry more than one passenger because of official pressure to encourage car pooling. Employees from outlying areas have been especially attracted to car-pooling, and van pools have become a common sight. To their actual travel time, many employees who arrive by car have to add up to 15 minutes of walking time between their cars and their offices twice a day. Parking permits other than for car pools are issued on the basis of rank; location of a parking place is generally a sign of status.

Once the road system was completed in 1943, District of Columbia and Virginia bus systems provided efficient transportation for thousands of riders daily. In March 1943, shortly after the building was completed, the War Department announced that about half of Pentagon workers used buses. It was claimed that the bus lanes under the building could handle 25,000 passengers per hour and that as many as 28 buses could be loaded at the same time. Buses provided most of the transport for Pentagon workers for the first 35 years and thereafter supplemented Metrorail. Easy access to the building via stairways to the Concourse greatly facilitated the flow of passenger traffic.

The coming of the Metro system to the Pentagon in 1977 brought with it a number of changes. From its deep underground station, the Metro introduced an even larger volume of workers into the Concourse, the chief outlet from the station and from the bus terminal also. This greater density may have been a factor in the decision some years later to close off part of the Concourse to the public and impose tighter security control over access to the building. For readier access to the Metro, between 1976 and 1978, the bus terminal was moved above ground to the Concourse side of the building nearest the Metro. The tunnels continued to be used by taxis until 1985 when they were closed for security reasons and subsequently converted to office space.

The Metro also made it possible to diminish the use of government vehicles for local business use. Metro fare cards issued to offices in the Pentagon and other Department of Defense buildings could be used to reach many locations not previously readily accessible by public transportation. Measured against the scale of overall Defense expenditures this was a minor economy, but it was a step in the right direction.

North Parking, end of the day

The National Military Command Center in the Pentagon is the primary component of the command and control system. In 1965 it occupied 30,000 square feet of space. An expanded facility, constructed at a cost of $15.4 million and containing 77,000 square feet, opened in February 1976. It housed the U.S. terminus of the "hot line" with Moscow which permitted swift communication between the governments of the United States and the Soviet Union. NMCC watch teams, under officers of general/admiral rank, are continuously on duty to provide constant coordination and liaison with the White House, State Department, other U.S. government agencies, and NATO. The NMCC has extensive communications and other electronic equipment, crisis management facilities, modern graphic information displays, and accommodations for additional crisis watch personnel as needed.

The Conference Management Table (CMT) in Emergency Conference Room (ECR) of the National Military Command Center (NMCC)

The perceived need for better and still more rapid coordination of decisionmaking at the secretary of defense level became more urgent as a result of unsatisfactory experiences with military exercises and crisis situations during the later 1970s and early 1980s. In 1986-88 a new 5,200 sq. ft. Crisis Coordination Center was constructed near the immediate office of the secretary of defense and adjacent to the NMCC. Equipped with a network of computer terminals and secure telephones, the center receives from the Joint Chiefs of Staff and other DoD elements information about crises anywhere in the world, enabling the DoD leadership to make quick and informed policy and action decisions. The center operates on a normal work week schedule except in times of crisis, when it operates on a 24-hour basis with a greatly expanded staff. The effectiveness of the system was thoroughly tested in 1990-91 during the Desert Shield/Desert Storm deployment and operations in the Persian Gulf area.

Crime within the building has included many of the forms that occur in large urban areas. The most frequent have been petty thievery and pilferage of government equipment—especially office equipment, and particularly computers. It is likely that the cost to the government of this loss is hundreds of thousands of dollars per year. Prior to the advent of government-sponsored lotteries in the adjacent area—Virginia, Maryland, and the District of Columbia—numbers-running was common in the building. Other crimes include forgery, fraud, burglary, gambling, embezzlement, and assault. Homicide has been rare.

Enforcement of traffic and parking regulations is an important function because of the huge volume of traffic and the pressures for parking space that never seems to be adequate to meet needs. Hundreds of violations and a number of accidents occur each month. Until recent years, failure to pay fines for parking citations could lead to arrest of offenders in the building by U.S. marshals and their transport (sometimes in handcuffs) to federal court in Alexandria. This form of enforcement was replaced by simply towing the cars of offenders to a lot, originally some dozen miles from the building but more recently in the Pentagon North Parking area. On the average, perhaps 250 cars are towed each month. The need for traffic patrols is constant. Efforts to diminish the volume of traffic and parking by encouraging car pools and greater use of public transportation have helped, but the coming and going of more than 10,000 cars daily requires perpetual attention and law enforcement.

Entrance from Metro underground and buses, 1990

Demonstrations

The quintessential symbol of war and the U.S. military establishment, the Pentagon became the preferred field of action, sometimes violent, for demonstrations by pacifist, antimilitary, and antiwar groups. Protest rallies have been held frequently outside of the Pentagon and, at times, in the Concourse, before that area was closed off to the public in 1985. Most of these demonstrations have been peaceful; protesters generally confined themselves to conveying their messages through placards and verbal exhortations. It has often been necessary to remove obstructive demonstrators by force and to arraign them before a U.S. Commissioner in Alexandria, Virginia. Cases of a serious nature are presented to the U.S. District Court of Northern Virginia, also in Alexandria. The largest and most violent demonstrations occurred during the Vietnam War, which perhaps evoked more antiwar sentiment and certainly more demonstrations throughout the country than any war in U.S. history.

In October 1967 the National Mobilization Committee to End the War in Vietnam, a loose association of protest groups, sponsored and organized what it advertised as the largest antiwar rally in American history. It received official sanction for the rally for the 48-hour period, 21 and 22 October. Official estimates of the number of protesters ranged from 30,000 to 55,000, while the organizers claimed as many as 150,000 attended the initial rally at the Lincoln Memorial on Saturday, 21 October. From there, many of the protesters, estimated by the Army at 25,000, marched to the Pentagon, some with the avowed purpose of disrupting Pentagon activities and gaining entrance to the building. The permit for the rally required that the protesters confine their activities to the North Parking area and an area opposite the Mall Entrance.

An estimated 25,000 to 35,000 people assembled at the Pentagon in the afternoon and evening. To guard against efforts to gain entrance to the building, more than 1,200 military police and additional units from various bases around the country had been brought in, and U.S. marshals were on hand to make arrests if it became necessary. Other military units —principally a brigade task force of some 2,500 men from the 82nd Airborne Division—were held in reserve in the Washington area—at Andrews Air Force Base, Md.; Fort Meade, Md.; Fort Myer, Va.; Ft. Belvoir, Va.; and elsewhere. Protective cordons of troops, Pentagon police, and more than 200 marshals sought to fence off the area in which the ralliers were assembled.

Anti-Vietnam War demonstration at the Pentagon, October 1967

Attempts by protesters to pierce the military lines were repelled until about 5:40 p.m. when a large number of them, about 2,000, broke through to the building and sought to enter. About 30 got into the building through an unlocked door near the Mall Entrance; they were expelled by additional troops from inside the building, and marshals arrested some of them. Others threw rocks and bottles at the building and the soldiers, broke windows, and scrawled graffiti on the walls. The soldiers pushed the crowds back and strong reactions led to injuries on both sides. Tear gas, which may have been released by soldiers and/or by demonstrators who grabbed grenades from soldiers, had some deterrent effect on the crowd. Most of the crowd dispersed during the evening, but a number of demonstrators spent the night outside the building and planned to resume the protest on Sunday, when they were joined by additional hundreds.

The confrontation by much smaller numbers than on the previous day continued throughout Sunday, during which more arrests occurred. When the permit for the demonstration expired at midnight, demonstrators who refused to leave the area were arrested. In all there were more than 660 arrests over the weekend. The usual penalty was a fine and a suspended sentence. The 45 persons reported injured were almost evenly divided between demonstrators (21) and law enforcers (15 marshals and 9 soldiers). The leaders of the demonstration claimed a "tremendous victory." Beyond question they succeeded in gaining the attention of the government, the whole country, and perhaps much of the rest of the world.

Subsequent demonstrations at the Pentagon did not approach the 1967 march in size or intensity. In May 1971 some demonstrators attempted a march on the Pentagon from Washington but were turned back and arrested before they reached the building. They were part of a much larger gathering between 3 and 5 May—estimated at 30,000—that sought to close down the government by blocking entrances to government buildings in Washington and massing in streets to disrupt traffic. Police and federal troops thwarted this effort and more than 7,000 demonstrators were arrested.

After the Vietnam War, antiwar protests continued aimed chiefly at the existence and potential use of nuclear weapons. The largest of these post-Vietnam demonstrations occurred on 28 April 1980 during the Iranian crisis and after the attempt to rescue the American hostages in Iran. Some 1,200 anti-nuclear war activists marched on the Pentagon, where they threw blood and ashes on walls and blocked entrances. As many as 350 protesters were arrested. At another demonstration in 1982, 100 nuclear protesters ringed entrances and threw blood on columns; 28 were arrested in this incident.

1967 demonstration

Inhabitants

For its first five years of existence the Pentagon remained exclusively a War Department building and housed a large part of the departmental staff. Any notion that a single building could accommodate the whole staff, as General Craig and General Somervell had envisioned, vanished even before the Pentagon was completed and fully occupied in January 1943.

The arrival of Secretary of War Stimson and Chief of Staff Marshall in their Pentagon offices from the Munitions Building on 14 November 1942 may be regarded as the real opening of the Pentagon, although it was two months before the building's completion and six and a half months after the first arrivals. Stimson and Marshall occupied adjacent offices on the third floor in the E ring above the River Entrance; a connecting door permitted the Chief of Staff ready access to the secretary. Principal staff assistants occupied other "front offices" in the immediate area on the E ring. Under Secretary of War Patterson, the logistical chief of the War Department, had offices above the Mall Entrance; General Somervell, Commanding General of the Army Service Forces, had adjacent offices.

Before the Pentagon was fully occupied, General Marshall proposed that the Navy Department share the building with the War Department; he offered a million square feet of space to accommodate the top echelons of the Navy staff. Secretary of the Navy Frank Knox, favorably disposed toward the proposal, announced his acceptance early in November 1942. The Navy would take over all of the second floor and part of another to house at least 5,000 Navy Department employees and perhaps as many as 10,000. Knox had hoped to move in by 1 December, but he had failed to reckon with the opposition of Navy bureau chiefs, some of whom demanded more space and some of whom did not want to set up shop in the Pentagon. Marshall lost patience, and Stimson pointed out to the Navy that if its demand were met, it would have a larger percentage of its Washington staff in the Pentagon than would the Army. When the Navy persisted, Stimson decided to let the matter drop. By 1 December Knox had been forced to concede publicly that the move was impracticable.

It is doubtful that the uniformed Navy leaders wanted to move into the Pentagon. They cherished their independence as a separate service and saw no advantage to living cheek by jowl with the Army and the Army Air Forces. Moreover, they argued that to install the complex Navy communications system in the new building would require a lot of space and considerable time and the changeover might therefore impair the war effort. In his biography of General Marshall, historian Forrest Pogue noted that, ironically, the "Army had revenge of a sort, for the public assumed that all of the services were operating from the Pentagon. The building became so identified with the war that many later writers had difficulty realizing that it was not there from the beginning. As a result, occasional subsequent accounts of the attack at Pearl Harbor had officers rushing up and down in confusion in the fabled—and then uncompleted—Pentagon maze."

Left, Chief of Staff General of the Army George C. Marshall

An interesting phenomenon has been the consistency in the number of military personnel authorized for the Pentagon. Since 1945 this number has varied from about 9,500 to 13,500; most of the time it has been between 10,000 and 12,000. By contrast, authorized civilian personnel strength has ranged from about 11,000 to more than 18,000. Civilians have outnumbered military consistently, most heavily during periods of high occupancy, especially in wartime.

The War Department had the Pentagon to itself until the creation of the National Military Establishment in 1947 when it came under the secretary of defense. At that time the Army Air Forces separated from the Army and became the U.S. Air Force under the Department of Air Force, which took over its part of the building from its parent, now redesignated Department of the Army.

The Joint Chiefs of Staff moved to the New War Department Building in January 1946 and from there to the Pentagon in April 1947. The chiefs and their Joint Staff occupied a large portion of the second floor and some of the first floor in the Pentagon. As the staff grew in size over the years, from 277 in 1947 to 1,510 at the end of 1991, it required more space. The JCS conference room on the second floor has become famous as "The Tank," a name whose origin is sometimes traced to the initial meeting room in 1942, when the chiefs occupied the U.S. Public Health Building on Constitution Avenue. The entrance to that conference room was down a flight of stairs and through an archway that gave the impression of entering a tank. More recently, the JCS conference room in the Pentagon has become known also as "The Gold Room" because of the color of the carpeting and the drapes. Here the Secretary of Defense and other officials meet with the Joint Chiefs; the main subgroups of the JCS also meet in this room.

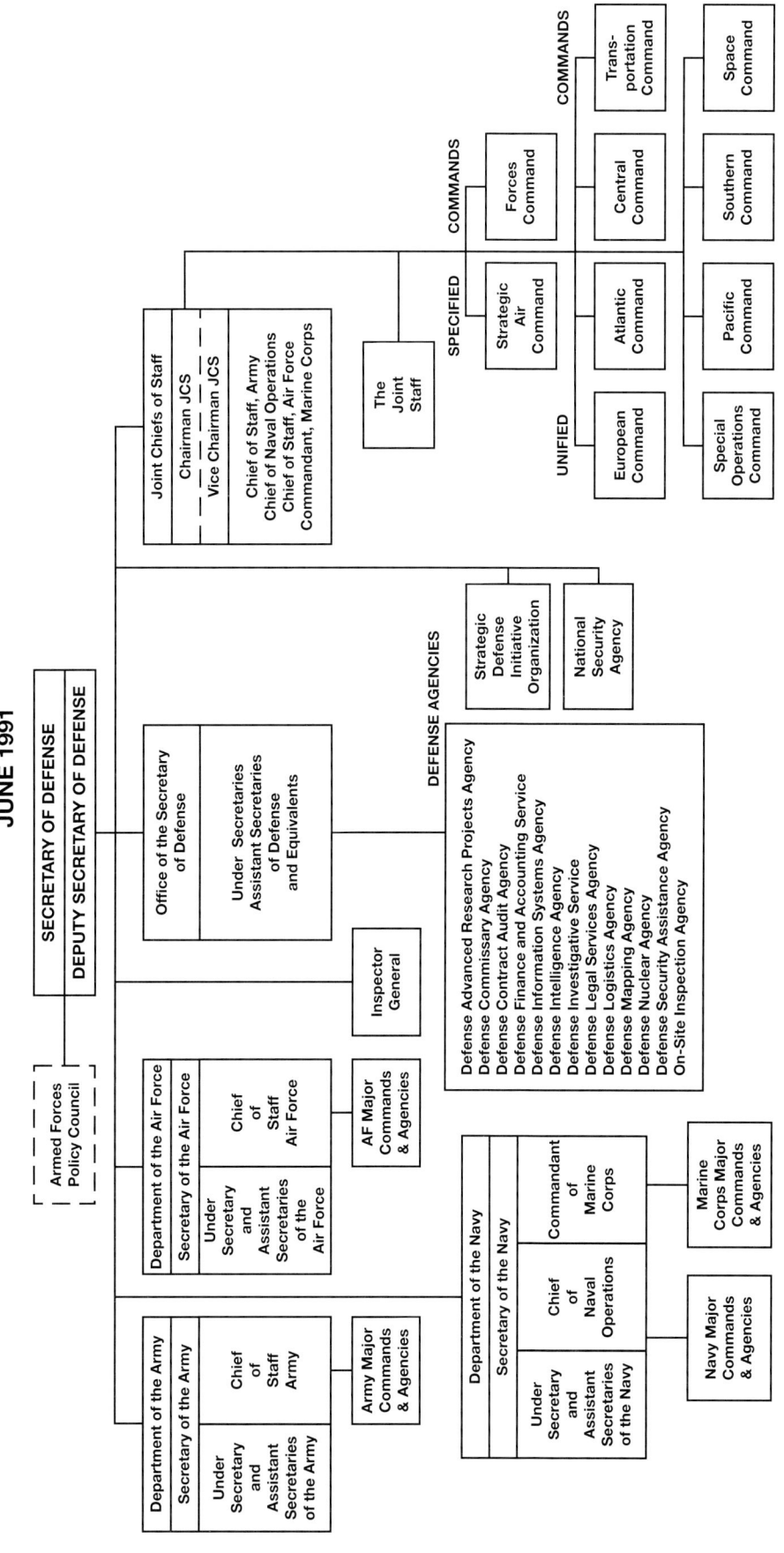

Secretary of Defense James Forrestal with Directors of Women's Services, left to right– Col. Geraldine P. May, Air Force; Col. Mary A. Hallaren, Army; Capt. Joy Bright Hancock, Navy; Maj. Julia E. Hamblet, Marine Corps, 1948

The first Secretary of Defense, James Forrestal, moved into the Pentagon on 22 September 1947 and began the task of building a staff to help him. In time, the Office of the Secretary of Defense grew to more than 2,000 people, civilian and military, and came to occupy a substantial part of the building. Because of the continually growing number of high-ranking officials, OSD and some of its agencies and services occupied an amount of the building's space disproportionate to their personnel strength.

The Navy Department waited for almost a year after Forrestal took over to join the team in the Pentagon. Under Secretary of the Navy W. John Kenney moved into the building on 11 August 1948, followed at the end of the month by Secretary of the Navy John L. Sullivan, Chief of Naval Operations Admiral Louis Denfeld, and a large part of the Navy staff. The Navy initially received 300,000 square feet of office space, requiring the transfer of some 2,500 Army employees from the building. It received additional space the next year, but much of its staff remained in other buildings in the area. The Marine Corps Headquarters never did move into the Pentagon, perhaps because of what it considered lack of adequate space or because of a preference for separateness. In any event, it occupied the nearby large Navy Annex Building, overlooking the Pentagon and Arlington Cemetery and very close to the Marine Barracks at Henderson Hall.

Washington Star cartoon, 1947

When Forrestal moved into the Pentagon he did not take for himself the office occupied by Secretary of the Army Kenneth Royall but contented himself with a lesser office—that of the Under Secretary of the Army. Forrestal's successor, Louis Johnson, as one of his first acts in April 1949, exercised his prerogative of rank and took over the prime suite of offices from the Secretary of the Army. This suite, originally occupied by Secretary of War Stimson in 1942, included, in addition to an 880 sq. ft. office, a dining room, a kitchenette, bathroom, emergency living quarters, and a private elevator to the parking garage in the basement.

The deputy secretary of defense, a position created by law in August 1949, took over the office formerly occupied by General Marshall and General Dwight D. Eisenhower and in 1949 occupied by Army Chief of Staff General Omar N. Bradley. The Air Force and Navy secretaries and military chiefs inhabited offices in the E ring of the fourth floor, and their staffs had offices on the fifth floor also. The Joint Chiefs' domain was on the second floor in a sealed area with limited access and tight security. This arrangement, with minor changes chiefly to accommodate growth of OSD and JCS needs, remained constant in the years that followed.

The office of the secretary of defense

Before the building reached completion in January 1943, it had become clear that it would not be able to house the rapidly multiplying War Department work force. Although numbers ranging up to 33,000 worked in the building during the rest of the war (some of them on second and third shifts), the department retained many of its other buildings, including the New War Department Building and part of the Munitions Building. Moreover, additional temporary buildings were erected on the Mall and elsewhere in the city and in Northern Virginia. An Army (including an Army Air Forces of 2.4 million) that reached 8.2 million people at its peak in 1945 required a staff of many tens of thousands of military and civilians in Washington, occupying more than 30 buildings in addition to the Pentagon.

After the precipitate postwar demobilization, the Army shrank to a strength of little more than 550,000 by mid-1948; the new Air Force had fewer than 400,000 officers and men. The population of the Pentagon also declined, but not as much as might have been expected, because as other Army real estate holdings were closed or otherwise disposed of, many offices moved into the Pentagon to fill space made vacant. At the end of 1948, the Pentagon's population numbered more than 25,000, including some 2,000 non-Defense employees. The coming of the Korean War in June 1950 triggered another immediate increase in Pentagon people—in December 1950 they numbered more than 31,000, of whom 28,000 were Defense employees. After reaching a peak of more than 33,000 occupants in December 1952 the building's population declined gradually to about 29,000 in December 1960. The Vietnam War witnessed another rise to more than 31,000 in December 1970. Thereafter the number fluctuated between 25,000 and 27,000. (See Appendix II).

Secretary of Navy Frank Knox, 1942

Pentagon Profiles 165

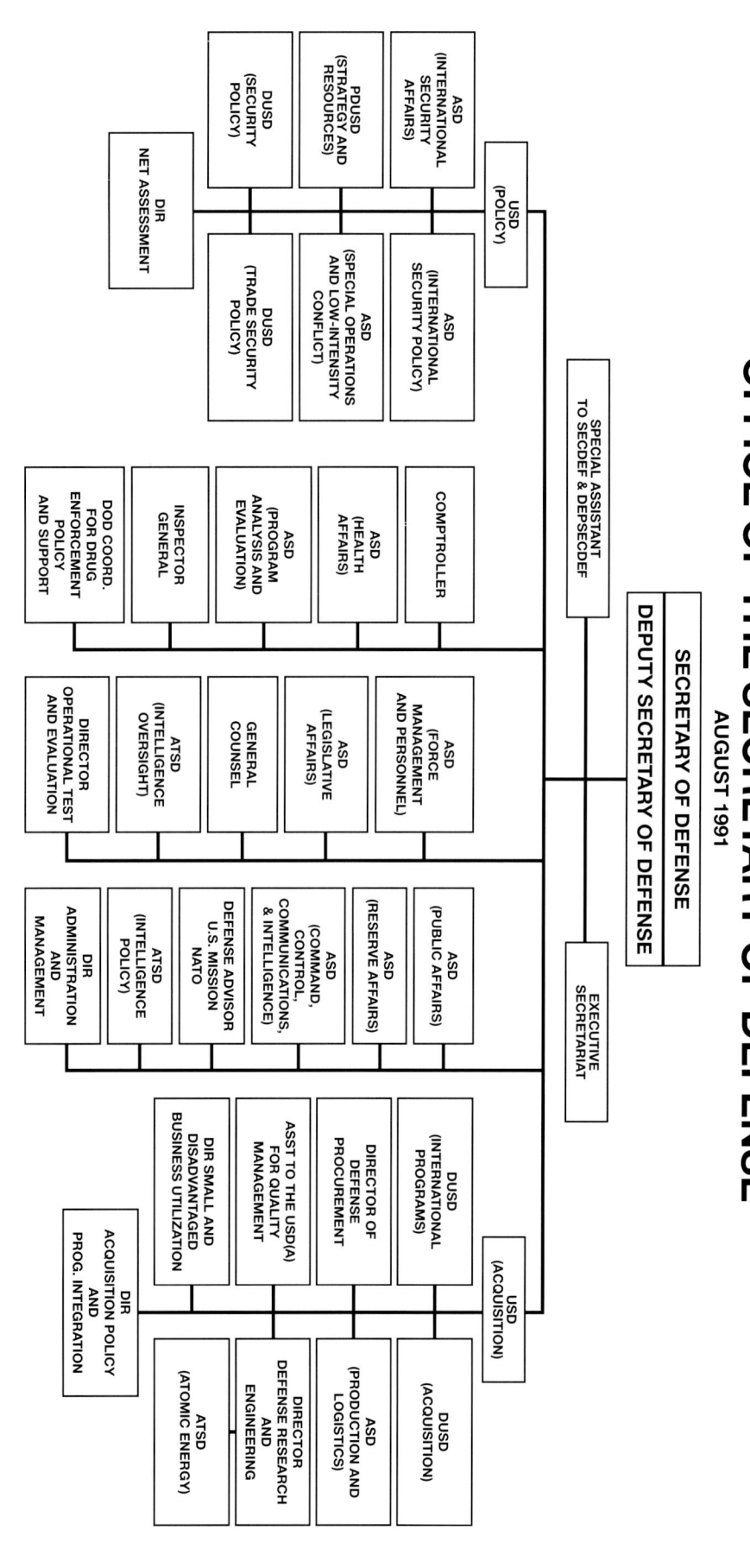

166 Pentagon Profiles

General Colin L. Powell, Chairman of the Joint Chiefs of Staff, 1989 –

Secretary of Defense Richard B. Cheney, 1989 –

Ceremony for King Saud of Saudi Arabia, Secretary of Defense Charles E. Wilson in center, 1957

President-elect Dwight D. Eisenhower at Pentagon with Secretary of Defense Robert A. Lovett and Chairman of Joint Chiefs of Staff Gen. Omar N. Bradley, 1952

*Secretary of Defense Robert A. Lovett
with Winston Churchill, 1952*

Secretary of Defense George C. Marshall and Assistant Secretary of Defense Anna Rosenberg, 1951

President Harry S. Truman with General Omar Bradley and Secretary of Defense Louis A. Johnson, 1949

Secretary of Defense Forrestal with, left to right, Secretary of the Army Kenneth Royall, Secretary of the Air Force Stuart Symington, and Secretary of the Navy John Sullivan, 1948

River Entrance

Pentagon Lore

The Pentagon entered into American folklore even before it was completed. During its construction there evolved a pastiche of fact, fiction, myth, whimsy, illusion, and fantasy that created a folklore of humor, black humor, and hostility that has endured and continued to grow for a half century. Amusing stories about the building began circulating from the earliest days of occupancy, many of them inspired by its vast expanse. An official publication in 1944 observed that the Pentagon had quickly "gained a reputation as the latest word in modern elaboration of the Labyrinth." The building had already inspired "humorous stories on a scale to rival the jeep or the Model T Ford car"; it was "an ideal hook on which to hang any tale which involves long journeys, losing one's way, crowds, confusion, massive walls, and bureaucratic red tape." The publication pronounced the Pentagon to be "simple, convenient, economical, and generally efficient in operation . . . getting lost in the building actually requires a special gift for bewilderment."

Names and epithets abounded. A favorite in the early years was "Somervell's Folly" but, like "Seward's Folly" (the U.S. purchase of Alaska from Russia in 1867), it lost its bite as time vindicated Somervell's initiative. *Life* called the Pentagon a "Cecil B. DeMille backdrop, 'a colossal pain in the neck' to everyone but Secretary of War Henry L. Stimson." This was unfair to Stimson, who had no special liking for the building. *Time*, on the other hand, in a more serious vein called it the "brain of U.S. armed might."

Inhabitants of the building, particularly the military, coined names for it that were often pejorative. *Five-Sided Wailing Wall*, *Five-Sided Squirrel Cage*, and *Five-Sided Funny Farm* all played on the polygon theme. Exasperation and disdain on the part of unhappy occupants, sometimes alleviated by a modicum of affection, gave rise to *Fort Fumble*, *The Fudge Factory*, *Potomac Puzzle Palace*, *Disneyland East*, and *White Elephant*.

Stories, humorous and otherwise, about the Pentagon invariably relate, in some way or other, to the construction and giant size of the building. One of the earliest favorites had to do with the Western Union messenger boy who entered the building on a Friday and emerged on Monday as a lieutenant colonel. Another story concerns a repairman who was sent to fix a connection in the ceiling on the third floor. He disappeared through a trap door and did not appear again until several days later when he staggered out onto an escalator on which General Marshall was riding. The theme of the lost wanderer received an international touch with the tale of French General Henri Giraud, who had escaped twice from German prisoner-of-war camps. Giraud had to find a guard to lead him out of the Pentagon. And in 1989, Secretary of Defense Richard Cheney, on one of his first days in office, became lost in the basement of the building and wandered for 10 minutes before finding his way out.

Environmental Impact

As early as January 1943, even before the completion of the building, an architectural commentary on the Pentagon pointed out its significant impact on the region around it—"the reclaimed slums, the broad roads, and the new integrated approaches to the capital." The Pentagon proved, indeed, to be a key catalyst for the transformation over a period of several decades of a near-bucolic landscape into a vast urban complex. The urbanization of Northern Virginia* increased its population more than eightfold (from 170,000 to more than 1,400,000) by 1990; during the same period the national population increased less than 100 percent. From the process emerged a major new economic and political center in the state of Virginia.

Requirements for housing and transportation for the Pentagon's workers stimulated the construction during the war of large garden-type apartment complexes in Arlington, each housing thousands of people. Unlike in the District of Columbia, large tracts of undeveloped land were available for construction. The Navy Annex, which had 7,300 workers, and the National Airport also contributed significantly to these requirements. Between 1940 and 1950 the population of the area doubled. With the increase in residential population came commercial growth which, together with some additional government installations, intensified the need for facilities of all kinds.

The Korean War provided strong impetus to development as the Pentagon increased its payroll and acquired and leased other facilities in Northern Virginia for its expanding work force. From this time on, the area experienced a steady large-scale growth of office buildings, commercial centers, housing of all kinds, roads, and transportation systems. While the federal government remained the largest employer, many research and industrial companies established themselves in Northern Virginia. Many other firms from around the country moved their headquarters into the area or established "Washington offices" in Arlington and Fairfax counties. The huge research and procurement programs of the Defense Department proved a particular attraction for many companies that found it convenient to be near the Pentagon.

The growth reached steadily outward from the Potomac as the closer-in areas of Arlington, Alexandria, Falls Church, and Fairfax became saturated. The skyline on the Virginia side of the Potomac reached ever higher as building height restrictions diminished; it greatly surpassed the subdued Washington skyline, where the only skyscraper was the Washington Monument. While the Defense Department remained the largest employer and perhaps the greatest magnet for attracting a wide variety of enterprises into the area, it no longer stood alone. The department had far more employees—civilian and military—in other buildings and installations in Northern Virginia than in the Pentagon. And instead of dominating its environment as it once did, the Pentagon now stands as only one, albeit still the largest, among many large structures along the Potomac.

*Including Arlington, Fairfax, Loudoun, and Prince William counties and the cities of Alexandria and Falls Church.

Left, South Entrance, 1990

ERECTED
1942
UNDER ACT OF CONGRESS
AUGUST 25 1941

Conclusion

Above and beyond the lore of humorous stories is the lore derived from the historic role the Pentagon played on the national and international stage for half a century. The men who directed the nation's military forces from the building and contributed so importantly to the making of national security policy shaped much of the history of the United States and the world. Leaders of the stature of George Marshall and Dwight D. Eisenhower were towering figures on the world stage.

From the Pentagon came the planning for and direction of the wars of the past half century—from World War II to the Persian Gulf conflict. Responsibility for the military aspects of the Cold War belonged to the Pentagon, and in the great crises of the period—most notably those involving Berlin and Cuba—the Pentagon was the command center. The Defense Department also played a vital humanitarian role during all of these years—assisting in the alleviation of the effects of civil disasters at home and abroad. These activities ranged from airlifting food, medicines, and supplies to victims of floods and earthquakes to fighting volcano eruptions and dropping feed to cattle stranded in snowstorms on the Great Plains. And with the end of the Cold War came the program for assistance to the Commonwealth of Independent States, the former republics of the Soviet Union.

During the next half century there will undoubtedly be numerous changes that will inspire new lore about the building. The coincidence of a completely renovated structure and a greatly altered world order may well evoke images of the U.S. military establishment that will differ from those of the past. In time, the Pentagon may indeed become as much a symbol for peacekeeping and assistance in civil emergencies as for warmaking. There can be little doubt that in the uncertain future, as in the past, the Pentagon will continue to be a notable maker of history.

Appendixes

Appendix I

Pentagon Facts

It should be understood that most of the statistical data presented below are approximate, even when the numbers are not rounded. Most of this data was compiled in the 1950s; changes in the building since have resulted in changes in the numbers, making it difficult to render precise figures. This is especially true of estimates of gross space and net space for offices, concessions, cafeterias, and storage, and parking space and capacity. Changes have also occurred in most other categories, including the number of restrooms, drinking fountains, electric clocks, light fixtures, and fire hose cabinets.

Floor space figures have been especially difficult to compute and should be regarded as informed estimates. An early and knowledgeable study of the Pentagon by the Control Division of the Army Services Forces in 1944 estimated gross floor space at 6,240,000 sq. ft. and "net rentable" space (offices, storage, garage, bus terminal, concourse, kitchens, cafeterias) at 4,395,879 sq. ft. Office space only was 3,634,489 sq. ft. Subsequent figures on gross floor space ranged from 6 million sq. ft. (1947) to 6,218,027 (1954), 6,546,360 (1979), and 6,500,000 (1991). Net or occupiable floor space ranged from 3,333,000 sq. ft. (1947) to 3,695,130 (1954), 3,705,397 (1979), and 3,800,000 (1991). The increases in net floor space after 1947 are credible because new occupiable space was created by enclosure of junctions of corridors at the A ring, of parts of ramps, and of sections of light courts, by extension of the mezzanine over additional parts of the basement, and by conversion of the bus lanes under the Concourse into offices. The high figure in 1944 is probably the result of the inclusion of areas as occupiable that were not included in later computations.

The task of attempting to compile precise data in a building as large as the Pentagon and keeping them up to date is, indeed, formidable.

Original total land area (acres) 583
    Government owned (acres) 296
    Purchased or condemned (acres) 287
        Cost $2,245,000
Current land area - 1992 (acres) 280
Area covered by Pentagon building (acres) 29
Area of center court (acres) 5
Area of heating and refrigeration plant (acres) 1
Area of sewage structures (acres) 1
Access highways built (miles) 30
Overpasses and bridges built 21
Parking space (acres) 67
    Capacity (vehicles) 9,500
Total cost of Pentagon project (including outside facilities) $85,000,000

The Pentagon Building Proper

Gross floor area (sq. ft.) 6,500,000

Net space for offices, concessions and storage (sq. ft.) 3,800,000

Cubic contents (cu. ft.) 77,025,000

Length of each outer wall (ft.) 921

Circumference 4,605

Height of building (ft.) ....71' 3½"

Number of floors ....5, plus mezzanine and basement

Total length of corridors (miles) 17½

Number of:

    Stairways 150

    Escalators 19

    Elevators 13

    Fire hose cabinets 672

    Restrooms 280

    Plumbing fixtures 4,900

    Drinking fountains 685

    Clocks installed 4,200

    Light fixtures 85,000

    Windows 7,748

Appendix II

Population of the Pentagon: 1942-1990

		Total*	War Department
War Department	Dec 31, 1942	23,293	21,474
	1943	29,734	27,874
	1944	30,904	29,625
	1945	26,548	25,455
	1946	22,718	21,625
			DoD
DoD	1948	23,884	22,876
	1950	29,793	28,221
	1952	31,419	29,643
	1955	29,780	28,860
	1960	27,115	26,190
	1965	26,770	25,845
	1970	29,352	28,350
	1975	25,287	25,264
	1980	23,341	23,326
	1985	24,154	24,106
	1990	25,324	25,269

* Totals include employees of other agencies, chiefly the Public Buildings Administration (1942-48) and the General Services Administration (1949-90). The above totals do not include about 2,000 additional persons working in the building.

Source: Prepared from statistical data supplied by General Services Administration.

Appendix III

Department of Defense
Active Duty Military Personnel: 1939–1990

Year	Total	Army	Navy	Marine Corps	Air Force
1939	334,473	189,839	125,202	19,432	
1940	458,365	269,023	160,997	28,345	
1941	1,801,101	1,462,315	284,427	54,359	
1942	3,858,791	3,075,608	640,570	142,613	
1943	9,044,745	6,994,472	1,741,750	308,523	
1944	11,451,719	7,994,750	2,981,365	475,604	
1945	12,055,884	8,266,373	3,319,586	469,925	
1946	3,024,893	1,435,496	978,203	155,679	455,515
1947	1,582,111	685,458	497,773	93,053	305,827
1948	1,444,283	554,030	417,535	84,988	387,730
1949	1,613,686	660,473	447,901	85,965	419,347
1950	1,459,462	593,167	380,739	74,279	411,277
1951	3,249,371	1,531,774	736,596	192,620	788,381
1952	3,635,912	1,596,419	824,265	231,967	983,261
1953	3,555,067	1,533,815	794,440	249,219	977,593
1954	3,302,104	1,404,598	725,720	223,868	947,918
1955	2,935,107	1,109,296	660,695	205,170	959,946
1956	2,806,441	1,025,778	669,925	200,780	909,958
1957	2,794,761	997,994	676,071	200,861	919,835
1958	2,599,518	898,925	639,942	189,495	871,156
1959	2,503,631	861,964	625,661	175,571	840,435
1960	2,475,438	873,078	616,987	170,621	814,752
1961	2,482,905	858,622	626,223	176,909	821,151
1962	2,805,603	1,066,404	664,212	190,962	884,025
1963	2,698,927	975,916	663,897	189,683	869,431

Year	Total	Army	Navy	Marine Corps	Air Force
1964	2,685,782	973,238	665,969	189,777	856,798
1965	2,653,926	969,066	669,985	190,213	824,662
1966	3,092,175	1,199,784	743,322	261,716	887,353
1967	3,375,485	1,442,498	750,224	285,269	897,494
1968	3,546,071	1,570,343	763,626	307,252	904,850
1969	3,458,072	1,512,169	773,779	309,771	862,353
1970	3,064,760	1,322,548	691,126	259,737	791,349
1971	2,713,044	1,123,810	621,565	212,369	755,300
1972	2,321,959	810,960	586,923	198,238	725,838
1973	2,251,936	800,973	563,683	196,098	691,182
1974	2,162,005	783,330	545,903	188,802	643,970
1975	2,128,120	784,333	535,085	195,951	612,751
1976	2,081,910	779,417	524,678	192,399	585,416
1977	2,074,543	782,246	529,895	191,707	570,695
1978	2,061,708	771,624	529,557	190,815	569,712
1979	2,026,892	758,852	523,335	185,250	559,455
1980	2,050,627	777,036	527,153	188,469	557,969
1981	2,082,560	781,419	540,219	190,620	570,302
1982	2,108,612	780,391	552,996	192,380	582,845
1983	2,123,349	779,643	557,573	194,089	592,044
1984	2,138,157	780,180	564,638	196,214	597,125
1985	2,151,032	780,787	570,705	198,025	601,515
1986	2,169,112	780,980	581,119	198,814	608,199
1987	2,174,217	780,815	586,842	199,525	607,035
1988	2,138,213	771,847	592,570	197,350	576,446
1989	2,130,229	769,741	592,652	196,956	570,880
1990	2,043,705	732,403	579,417	196,652	535,233

Prepared By: Washington Headquarters Services
Directorate for Information
Operations and Reports

Appendix IV

Secretaries of War
1940–1947

Henry L. Stimson
Served in U.S. Army in World War I to rank of colonel. In private law practice much of career. Secretary of War, 1911-1913, Governor General of Philippine Islands, 1927-1929, Secretary of State, 1929-1933. Became Secretary of War for a second time and served through all of World War II, July 10, 1940 to September 21, 1945.

Robert P. Patterson
Lawyer and federal judge. Served with U.S. Army in France in World War I to rank of major. Assistant Secretary of War, July 1940-December 1940, and Under Secretary of War from December 1940 to September 1945. Secretary of War from September 27, 1945 to July 18,1947.

Kenneth C. Royall
Served in the U.S. Army in World Wars I and II. In private law practice, 1919-1942. Served as Under Secretary of War from November 9, 1945 until July 18, 1947, when he became Secretary of War. On September 18, 1947 he became the first Secretary of the Army and served until April 18, 1949.

Appendix V

Secretaries of Defense

James V. Forrestal

Except for serving briefly in World War I in the U.S. Navy, he was with Dillon, Read and Company from 1916 until 1940, when he became Under Secretary of the Navy, serving until May 1944, when he was appointed Secretary of the Navy. He left the Navy post on September 17, 1947, when he took the oath of office as the first Secretary of Defense, a position he kept until March 28, 1949. He died less than two months after leaving office.

Louis A. Johnson

After active service with the U.S. Army in France during World War I, he was a partner in the law firm of Steptoe and Johnson. He helped to found the American Legion and was its national commander in 1932-1933. He served as Assistant Secretary of War from June 1937 until July 1940. On March 28, 1949, he was sworn in as Secretary of Defense and served until September 19, 1950. He returned to law practice.

George C. Marshall

Commissioned in the U.S. Army in 1902, he rose to Chief of Staff in September 1939, serving thoughout World War II until November 1945. He was Secretary of State from 1947 to 1949, when he became president of the American Red Cross. He was sworn in as Secretary of Defense on September 21, 1950. This required a special congressional waiver because the National Security Act prohibited a military officer from serving as secretary if he had been on active duty within the previous 10 years. He served until September 12, 1951.

Robert A. Lovett

A Navy pilot in World War I with service overseas, he joined Brown Brothers Harriman and Co., eventually becoming a partner. He served as a special assistant to the Secretary of War beginning in December 1940 and then as Assistant Secretary of War for Air from April 1941 to December 1945. Was Under Secretary of State from July 1947 to January 1949, and Deputy Secretary of Defense, October 4, 1950, to September 16, 1951. He succeeded Marshall as Secretary of Defense on September 17, 1951, serving until January 20, 1953, at which time he returned to Brown Brothers Harriman and Co.

Charles E. Wilson

An electrical engineer, he became president in 1941 of General Motors Corp., with which he had been associated since 1929, and was still in that office when he was selected to be Secretary of Defense. He was sworn in as Secretary on January 28, 1953, and served until October 8, 1957.

Neil H. McElroy

Employed by Procter and Gamble from 1925, serving as president from 1948 to 1957. He was sworn in as Secretary of Defense on October 9, 1957, and resigned on December 1, 1959. Became chairman of the board at Procter and Gamble.

Thomas S. Gates, Jr.

Served in the U.S. Navy during World War II, in which he participated in campaigns in Europe and the Pacific. Was associated with Drexel and Co., 1925-1953. He was appointed Under Secretary of the Navy in October 1953, became Secretary of the Navy on April 1, 1957, and Deputy Secretary of Defense on June 8, 1959. He was sworn in as Secretary of Defense on December 2, 1959, and served until January 20, 1961. He joined Morgan and Company, becoming president in 1962.

Robert S. McNamara

Entered the U S. Army in 1943 and served until 1946. Held various offices in the Ford Motor Co. including president and director, from 1946 to 1961. Was sworn in as Secretary of Defense on January 21, 1961, and served until February 29, 1968. He became president of the World Bank in 1968.

Clark M. Clifford

Served in the U.S. Navy during World War II from 1944 to 1946, with assignment as naval aide to the President. Subsequently he served as special counsel to the President from 1946 until 1950. Became a partner in the law firm of Clifford and Miller in 1950. He was sworn in as Secretary of Defense on March 1, 1968, and served until January 20, 1969. Returned to law practice again.

Melvin R. Laird

Entered the U.S. Navy in 1942 and served in the Pacific; left the Navy in 1946. A former congressman from Wisconsin, 1953-1969, he was sworn in as Secretary of Defense on January 22, 1969, and served until January 29, 1973. Later, he became advisor to the President from June 1973 to February 1974, and then became senior counselor to *Reader's Digest*.

Elliot L. Richardson

Served in the U.S. Army in World War II, 1942-1945. Assistant Secretary of Health, Education, and Welfare, 1957-1959; Lieutenant Governor of Massachusetts, 1965-1967; and Under Secretary of State, 1969-1970. He was serving as Secretary of HEW, 1970-1973, when appointed Secretary of Defense. He was sworn in as Secretary of Defense on January 30, 1973, and served until May 24, 1973, then becoming U.S. Attorney General on May 25, 1973.

James R. Schlesinger

Had been at Rand Corporation from 1963 to 1967. He was assistant director of the Bureau of the Budget in 1969 and the Office of Management and Budget, 1970-1971. He served as Chairman of the Atomic Energy Commission, 1971-1973, and as Director of the Central Intelligence Agency in 1973. He was sworn in as Secretary of Defense on July 2, 1973, and served until November 19, 1975. Subsequently, he became the first Secretary of the new Department of Energy in October 1977 and served until July 1979.

Donald H. Rumsfeld

A U.S. Navy aviator and flight instructor in the 1950s, he was a Member of Congress from Illinois, 1963-1969, and became an assistant and counselor to President Nixon in 1969. He served as Director of the Office of Economic Opportunity and Director of the Cost of Living Council. Was U.S. Ambassador to NATO from 1973 to 1974, assistant to President Ford in 1974-1975, serving as director of the White House Office of Operations. He was sworn in as Secretary of Defense on November 20, 1975, and served until January 20, 1977. He became chief executive of G.D. Searle and Co.

Harold Brown

He was director of the Lawrence Livermore Laboratories in 1960 and then served as Director of Defense Research and Engineering, 1961-1965, and as Secretary of the Air Force, 1965 to 1969. He was president of the California Institute of Technology, 1969-1977. He was sworn in as Secretary of Defense on January 21, 1977, and served until January 20, 1981, when he joined the Johns Hopkins University School of Advanced International Studies.

Caspar Weinberger

During World War II he served in the U.S. Army and became a member of General MacArthur's intelligence staff. He was Director of the Office of Management and Budget, 1972-1973, and Secretary of Health, Education and Welfare from 1973 to 1975. He was general counsel, vice president, and director of the Bechtel Corp. from 1975 to 1981. He was sworn in as Secretary of Defense on January 21, 1981, and served until November 23, 1987.

Frank C. Carlucci

Served in the U.S. Navy, 1952-1954. Served as Director, Office of Economic Opportunity, 1970-1972; Under Secretary of HEW, 1972-1974; ambassador to Portugal, 1974-1978; deputy director of the CIA, 1978-1981. He was Deputy Secretary of Defense, 1981-1983, and was sworn in as Secretary of Defense on November 23, 1987, serving until January 20, 1989. (Deputy Secretary of Defense William H. Taft served as Acting Secretary of Defense from January 20, 1989 until March 20, 1989).

Richard B. Cheney

Served as special assistant to the Director of the Office of Economic opportunity, 1969-1970; as deputy to the presidential counselor, 1970-1971; as assistant director of operations of the Cost of Living Council, 1971-1973; and as Assistant to the President, 1975-1977. He was elected to Congress from Wyoming in 1978 and served until March 1989. He took the oath of office as Secretary of Defense on March 21, 1989.

Appendix VI

Joint Army and Air Force

Bulletin No. 23

DEPARTMENTS OF THE ARMY AND
THE AIR FORCE
Washington 25, D.C., 22 August 1949

SEAL, DEPARTMENT OF DEFENSE.—1. The following memorandum from the Secretary of Defense, 15 August 1949, is published for the information and guidance of all concerned:

In accordance with the provisions of Section 202 of the National Security Act of 1947, as amended by Section 5 of Public Law 216, 81st Congress, August 10, 1949, and with the approval of the President, the seal of the National Military Establishment is hereby redesignated as the seal for the Department of Defense with the change of designation. The design is redescribed as follows:

An American eagle is displayed facing to the right. Wings are horizontal. The eagle grasps three crossed arrows and bears on its breast a shield whose lower two-thirds carries alternating white and red stripes and whose upper third is blue. Above the eagle is an arc of thirteen stars with alternating rays. Below the eagle is a wreath of laurel extending to the eagle's right and wreath of olive extending to the eagle's left. On an encircling band is the inscription "Department of Defense" and "United States of America."

When the seal is displayed in color, the background is to be of medium blue with the eagle and wreath in natural colors and the arrows, stars, and rays of gold. The encircling band is to be dark blue with gold edges and letters in white.

The American bald eagle, long associated with symbolism representing the United States of America and its military establishment, has been selected as an emblem of strength. In facing to the right, the field of honor is indicated. The eagle is defending the United States, represented by the Shield of thirteen pieces. The thirteen pieces are joined together by the blue chief, representing the Congress. The rays and stars above the eagle signify glory, while the three arrows are collectively symbolic of the three component parts of the Department of Defense. The laurel stands for honors received in combat defending the peace represented by the olive branch.

LOUIS JOHNSON
Secretary of Defense

Note on Sources and Bibliography

The documents used in the preparation of this book came from diverse sources. The U.S. Army Office of the Chief of Engineers records are in the Washington National Records Center at Suitland, Md. in Record Group (RG) 77. A select group of Engineers' records are in the files of the Office of History, Headquarters, Army Corps of Engineers at Fort Belvoir, Va. These files contain a prime collection of primary source documents on the planning and construction of the Pentagon, interviews with key figures, and an extensive newspaper clipping file kept by Col. Clarence Renshaw. The records of the Office of the Quartermaster General, of which the Construction Division was a part until its transfer to the Engineers in December 1941, are in RG 92 at the National Archives and Records Administration. A collection of documents in the records of the U.S. Army Staff, RG 319, at the National Archives, entitled Supporting Documents to Historical Manuscript Collection, contains useful information about the building and its operation. Of great value also was the collection of documents and pictures assembled by David Witmer, one of the two chief architects of the Pentagon. This collection, donated to the government in 1991 by David Witmer's son Peter, is a small treasure trove of information about the building. The Witmer papers may be found in the National Archives and Records Administration. John Ohl's unpublished biography of Brehon B. Somervell provided excellent background information about Somervell and his role in the construction of the Pentagon.

Published primary sources used include the *Public Papers of Franklin D. Roosevelt*, *Papers of George Catlett Marshall*, and *Reports of the Secretary of War for 1939 and 1941*. Congressional publications provided valuable information, particularly the hearings of the House and Senate Appropriations Committees and their subcommittees in 1941.

A number of unpublished reports on the Pentagon were of exceptional interest. The Witmer Collection contains a study entitled "The Pentagon," dated September 1942 with no author attribution. It was probably prepared by a member or members of the architectural staff under Witmer. It contains plans, sketches, maps, pictures, statistical data, and an account of the construction of the building. Still another manuscript from the collection is entitled "Planning the Pentagon Building." Dated 21 October 1942, and possibly by Witmer, it contains important contemporary information. In August 1942, the Bureau of the Budget issued a "Report Covering Pentagon Building" which provided much useful data and a critical evaluation of the construction. A more comprehensive report, prepared at Somervell's behest by the Control Division of the Army Service Forces, appeared in June 1944. Entitled "The Pentagon Project," it presented a documented account of the history of construction, the cost, the highway system, and other aspects. Some time after World War II the Office of History of the Corps of Engineers produced a partial draft of a study entitled "The Pentagon Project." Although well-documented the draft was completed only up to the early stages of construction.

The OSD Historical Office provided extensive topical reference files containing DoD directives, memoranda, press releases, organizational materials, statistical data, manuals, and newspaper clippings. Over the years since 1944 the War Department, the Department of Defense, and the U.S. Army published information pamphlets about the Pentagon. The most complete and useful of these was the earliest, prepared by the Historical Branch of Army G-2 and published by the Pentagon Post Restaurant Council in December 1944. Particulars from this publication were especially useful in the preparation of Part II of this volume.

A technical report on the Pentagon Complex area by Daniel Koski-Karell provided much relevant information about the historical and archeological background of the region. Koski-Karell also prepared the basic data about the building to justify its nomination in 1989 to the National Register of Historic Places. This, too, contained useful information about the building as of the 1980s. Also helpful as the most recent reference source on the physical characteristics of the building was the *Status Report to the Congress on Renovation of the Pentagon*, prepared by the Office of the Secretary of Defense in 1991.

A number of secondary publications proved most helpful, especially *The Corps of Engineers: Construction in the United States* by Lenore Fine and Jesse Remington. John D. Millett's volume on the *Organization and Role of the Army Service Forces* and Forrest Pogue's *George C. Marshall, Organizer of Victory* also contained useful information. Articles in architectural and engineering journals, most of them contemporary with the period of the building's construction, contained much technical data and interesting observations about the design and construction of the Pentagon, particularly those in the *Architectural Forum* for September 1941 and January 1943 and *Engineering* for October 1942.

Many of the sources listed below and copies of most of the primary source documents are on file in the OSD Historical Office.

Government Publications

Annual Report of the Chief of Staff Malin J. Craig to the Secretary of War, in *Report of Secretary of War, FY 1939*.

Annual Report of the Secretary of War, FY 1941.

Department of Defense, Office of Public Affairs. *The Pentagon: A Description of the World's Largest Office Building*, n.d. but c. 1954.

Office of Secretary of Defense. *Renovation of the Pentagon*, 1 March 1991.

U.S. Congress, House Committee on Appropriations. *Hearings Before the Subcommittee on First Supplemental National Defense Appropriation Bill for 1942*, 77th Cong, 1st sess, 1941.

_____ _____. *Hearings on H.R. 5412, First Supplemental National Defense Appropriations Bill for 1942*, 77th Cong., 1st sess, 1941.

U.S. Congress, Senate Committee on Appropriations. *Hearings Before Subcommittee of the Committee on Appropriations on First Supplemental National Defense Appropriations Bill for 1942*, 77th Cong, 1st sess, 1941.

The Pentagon Post Restaurant Council. *The Pentagon*, Washington, D.C., n.d. but 1944-45.

U.S. Army Service Center for Armed Forces. *The Pentagon*, USASCAF Pamphlet No. 2 (Rev.), 1 June 1966.

Books

Adams, Henry H. *Harry Hopkins*. New York: Putnam, 1977.

Arnebeck, Bob. *Through A Fiery Trial*. Lanham, Md.: Madison Books, 1991.

Bagenul, Philip, and Jonathan Meades. *The Illustrated Atlas of the World's Great Buildings*. London: Salamander Books Ltd, 1980.

Burchard, Gary A. and Steve M. Pennington (eds). *Civil Engineering Landmarks in the Nation's Capital*. Washington, D.C.: American Society of Civil Engineers, 1982.

Burke, Lee H. *Homes of the Department of State, 1774-1976*. Washington, D.C.: Department of State, 1977.

Conn, Stetson, Ruth C. Engelman, and Byron Fairchild. *Guarding the United States and its Outposts*. Washington, D.C.: Office of the Chief of Military History, Department of the Army, 1964.

Cowdrey, Albert E. *A City For the Nation: The Army Engineers and the Building of Washington, D.C. 1790-1967*. Washington, D.C.: Office of the Chief of Engineers, U.S. Army Corps of Engineers, 1979.

Fine, Lenore, and Jesse Remington. *The Corps of Engineers: Construction in the United States*. Washington, D.C.: Office of the Chief of Military History, United States Army, 1972.

Green, Constance. *Washington, Capital City, 1879-1950*. Princeton, N.J.: Princeton University Press, 1963.

Gurney, Gene. *The Pentagon*. New York: Crown Publishers, Inc., 1964.

Hall, Scott. *Washington At War: 1941-1945*. Englewood Cliffs, N.J.: Prentice Hall, 1970.

James, Theodore, Jr. *The Empire State Building*. New York: Harper and Row, 1975.

Ketchum, Richard M. *The Borrowed Years, 1938-1941*. New York: Random House, 1989.

Kostof, Spiro. *America by Design*. New York: Oxford University Press, 1987.

McJimsey, George. *Harry Hopkins*. Cambridge, Mass.: Harvard University Press, 1987.

Millett, John D. *The Organization and Role of the Army Service Forces*. Washington, D.C.: Office of the Chief of Military History, Department of the Army, 1954.

Mollenhoff, Clark R. *The Pentagon*. New York: G.P. Putnam's Sons, 1967.

Pogue, Forrest C. *George C. Marshall, Organizer of Victory*. New York: Viking Press, 1973.

Rose, C.B., Jr. *Arlington County Virginia*. Arlington, Va.: Arlington Historical Society, 1976.

Scheips, Paul J., and M. Warner Stark. *Use of Troops in Civil Disturbances Since World War II*, Supplement II (1967). Washington, D.C.: Histories Division, Office of the Chief of Military History, Department of the Army, 1969.

Smith, Perry M. *Assignment: Pentagon*. Washington, D.C.: Pergamon-Brassey, 1987.

Tugwell, Rexford G. *The Democratic Roosevelt*. Garden City, N.Y.: Doubleday and Co., 1957.

Works Progress Administration. *Washington City and Capital*. American Guide Series, 1977.

Works Progress Administration, Washington, D.C. *A Guide to the Nation's Capital*. New York: Hastings House, 1942.

Articles

"Pentagon Building." *The Architectural Forum* (January 1943), 37-52.

"Planning the World's Largest Building." *Engineering* 129 (22 October 1942), 569-75.

Engineering News-Record (4 June 1942).

The Architectural Forum (September 1941), 2, 4.

Architectural Record (January 1943), 63-70.

McBane, Maj. Robert B. "The Pentagon Makes Sense." *Army Information Digest* (January 1947), 1-7.

Webb, Willard J. "Building The Pentagon In Arlington." *The Arlington Historical Magazine* (October 1984), 31-38.

Documentary Collections

Bland, Larry I., ed. *The Papers of George Catlett Marshall*, Vol. 2. Baltimore: The Johns Hopkins University Press, 1986.

———. *George C. Marshall: Interviews and Reminiscences for Forrest Pogue*. Lexington, Va.: George C. Marshall Research Foundation, 1991.

The Public Papers and Addresses of Franklin D. Roosevelt, 1941. New York: Harper and Bros. 1950. Samuel I. Rosenman, Compiler.

Interviews

Casey, Hugh J. Interviewed by John T. Greenwood, Office of History, Headquarters Army Corps of Engineers. 25-29 September 1979.

Clarke, Gilmore David. "The Reminiscences of." Oral History Research Office, Columbia University. 1960.

Connell, John. Washington, D.C. Interviewed by Alfred Goldberg. 18 December 1991.

Dougherty, Capt. Michael A. Interviewed by Alfred Goldberg. December 1991.

Freeman, L.W. Washington, D.C. Interviewed by Alfred Goldberg. 10 January 1992.

Leisenring, Luther. Washington, D.C. Interviewed by Jesse Remington and Lenore Fine, Office of History, Headquarters Army Corps of Engineers. 5 June 1957.

Mitchell, Maj. Paul. Interviewed by Alfred Goldberg. December 1991.

Renshaw, Col. Clarence. Interviewed by Jesse Remington and Lenore Fine, Office of History, Headquarters Army Corps of Engineers. 13 February 1959.

Reybold, Lt. Gen. Eugene. Interviewed by Jesse Remington and Lenore Fine, Office of History, Headquarters Army Corps of Engineers. 12 March 1959.

Williams, Betty. Washington, D.C. Interviewed by Alfred Goldberg. 12 December 1992.

Unpublished Materials

Koski-Karell, Daniel. Technical Report. Historical and Archaeological Background Research of the GSA Pentagon Complex Project Area. Submitted to David Volkert and Associates, Inc., Bethesda, Md., 3 January 1986.

National Register of Historic Places Inventory—Nomination Form for Federal Properties. Pentagon Office Building Complex. Prepared by Daniel Koski-Karell, Karell Archaeological Services, 15 June 1989.

Ohl, John. Brehon B. Somervell. (Full-scale biographical study.)